Wow!

CAN WE DO THAT AGAIN?

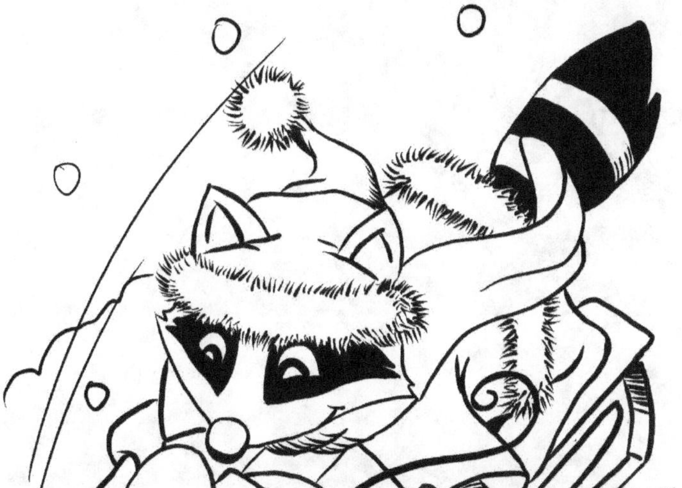

Coloring Book

BY JESS ERSKINE

WOW! CAN WE DO THAT AGAIN? COLORING BOOK

Rolling Donut Press
P.O. Box 1187
Canmer, KY. USA

www.RollingDonutPress.com

For all the children who love adventures.

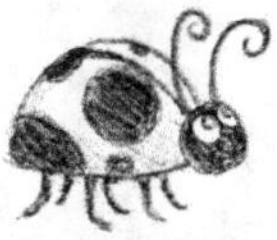

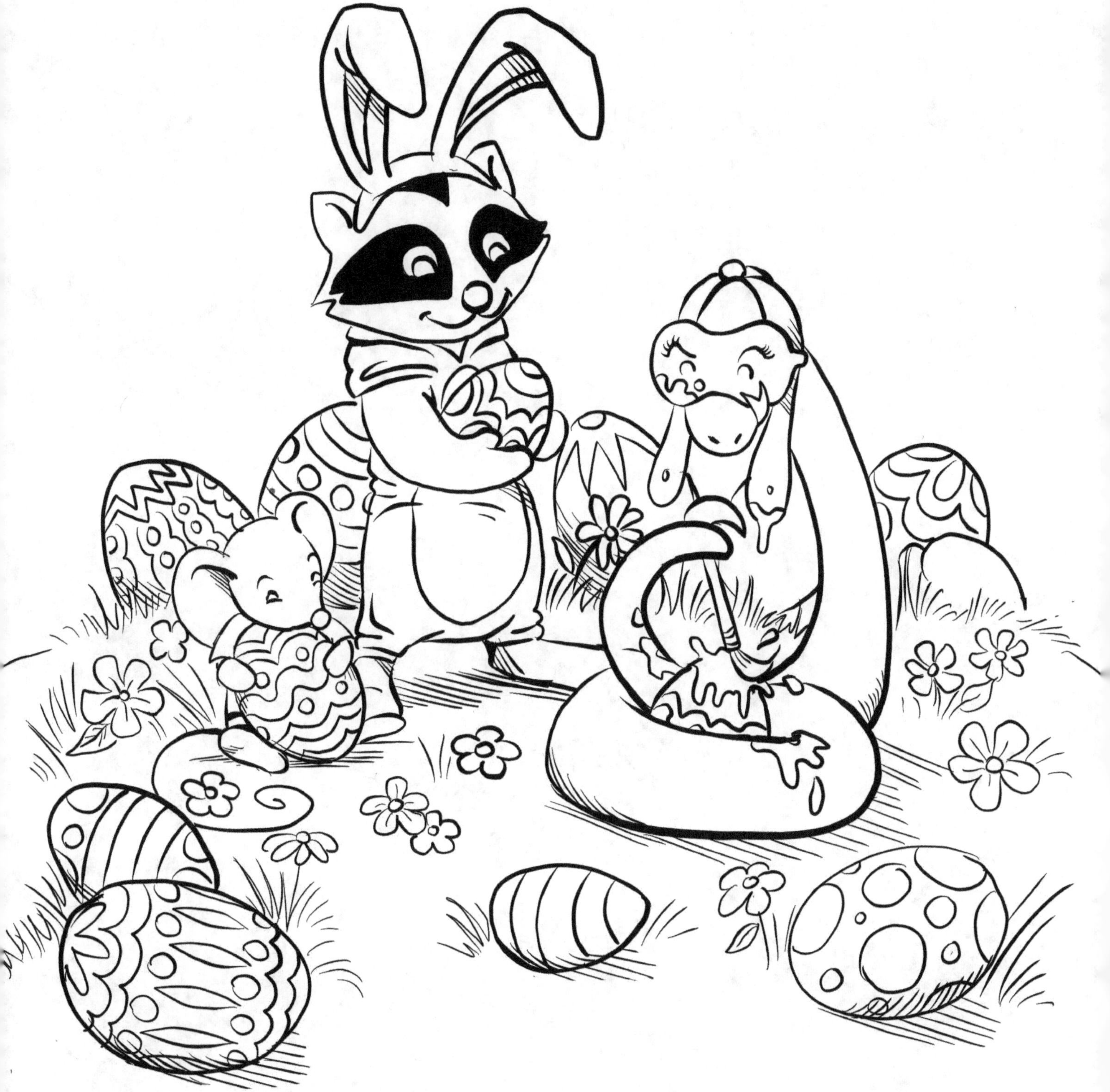

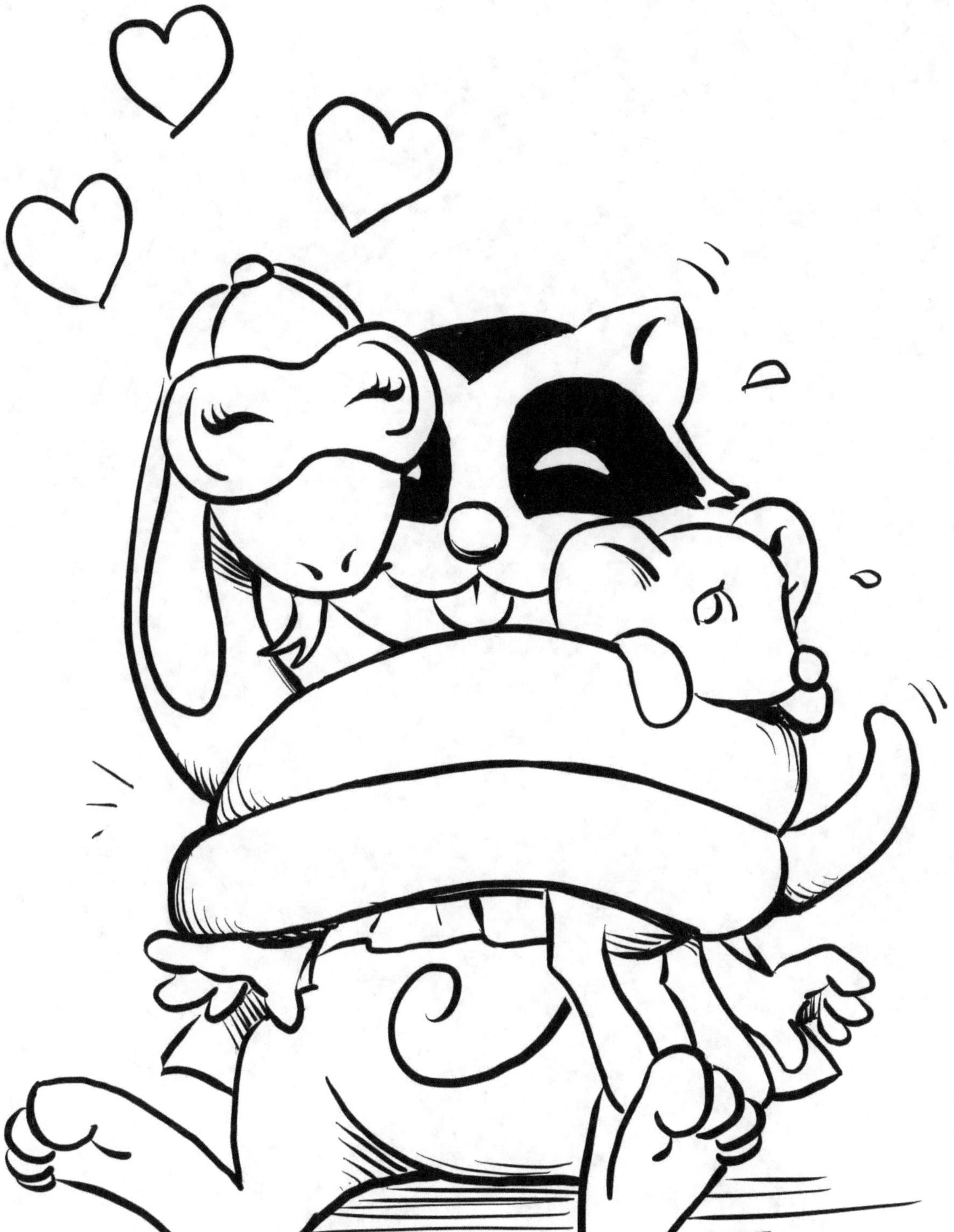

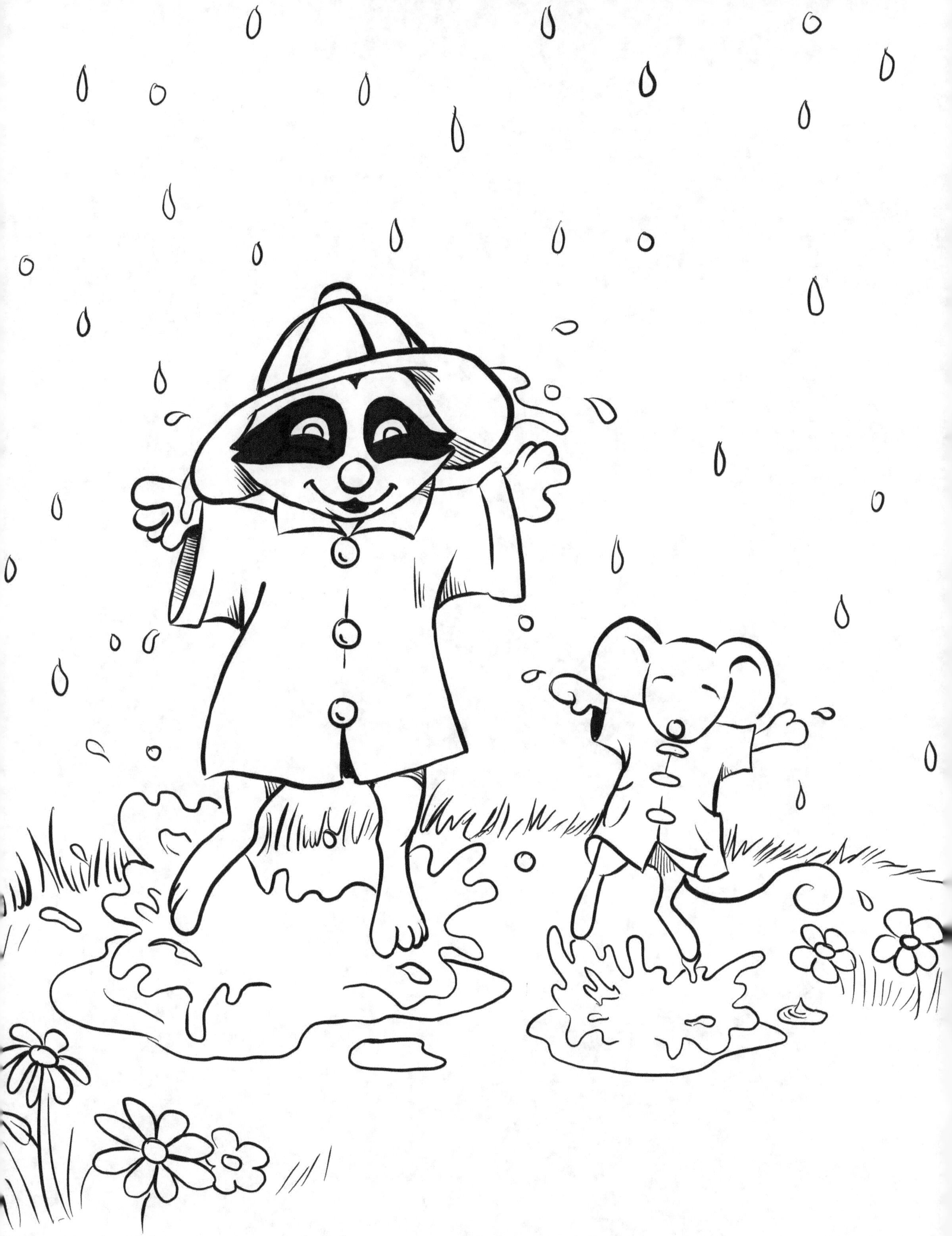

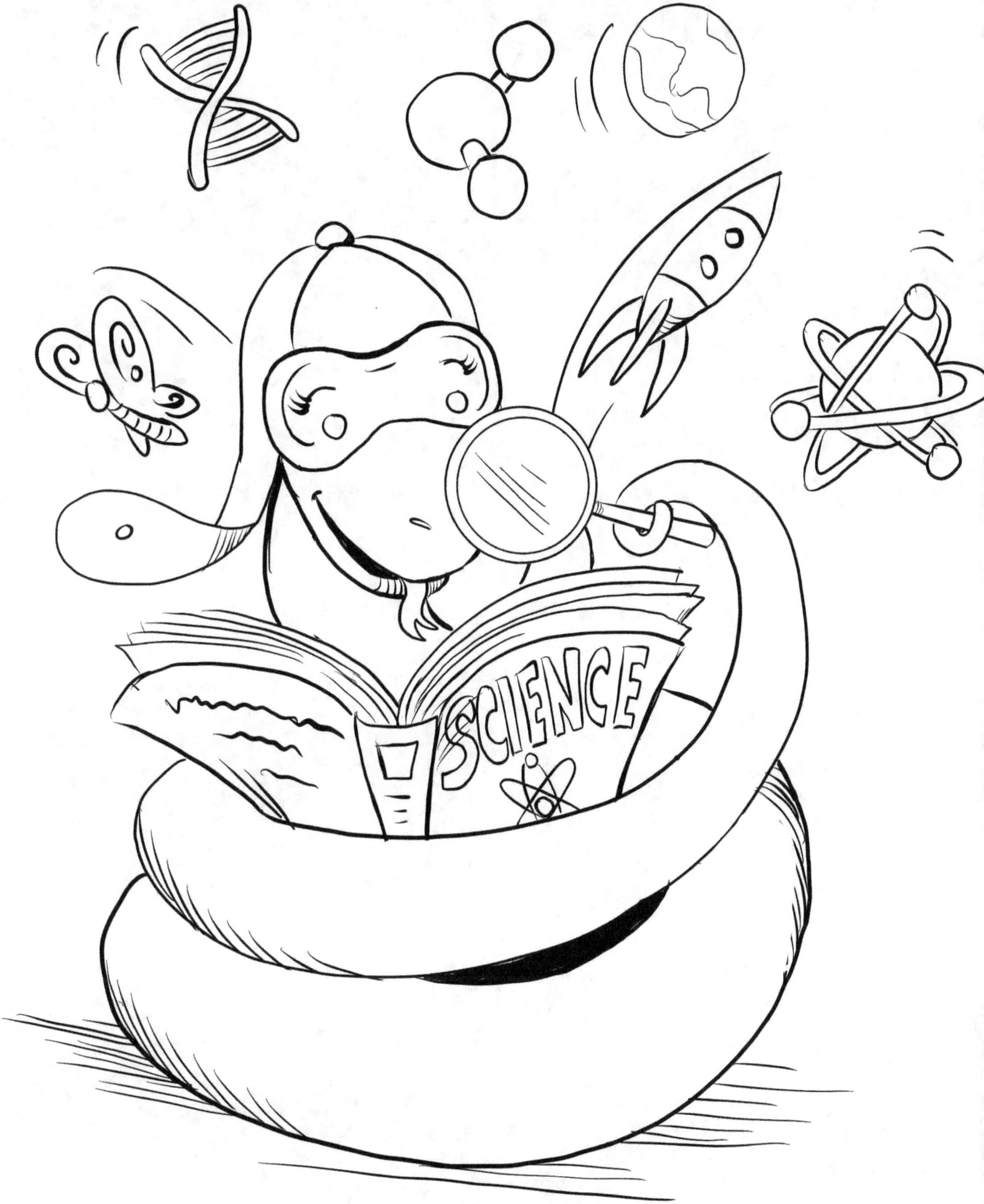
SCIENCE

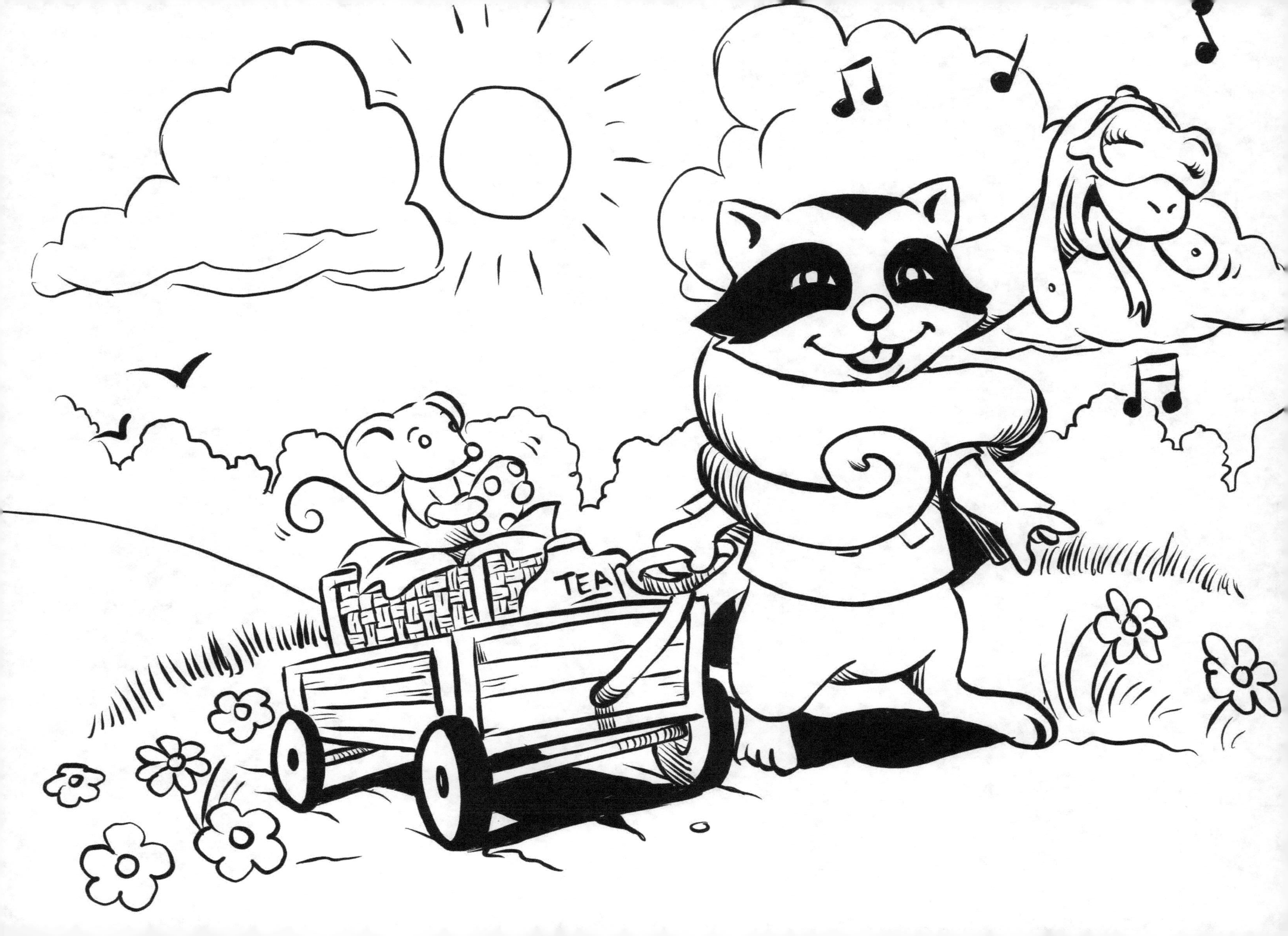
TEA

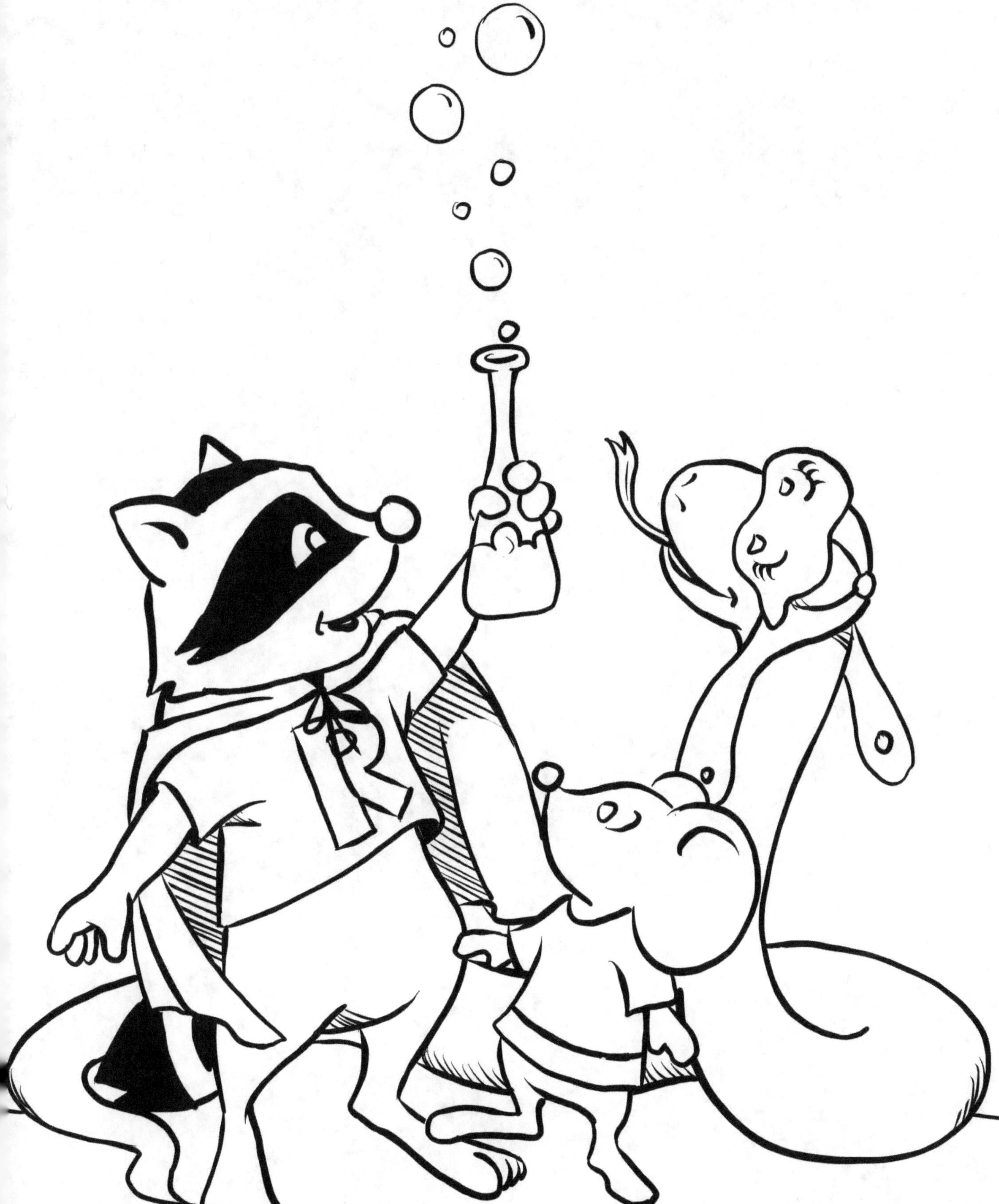

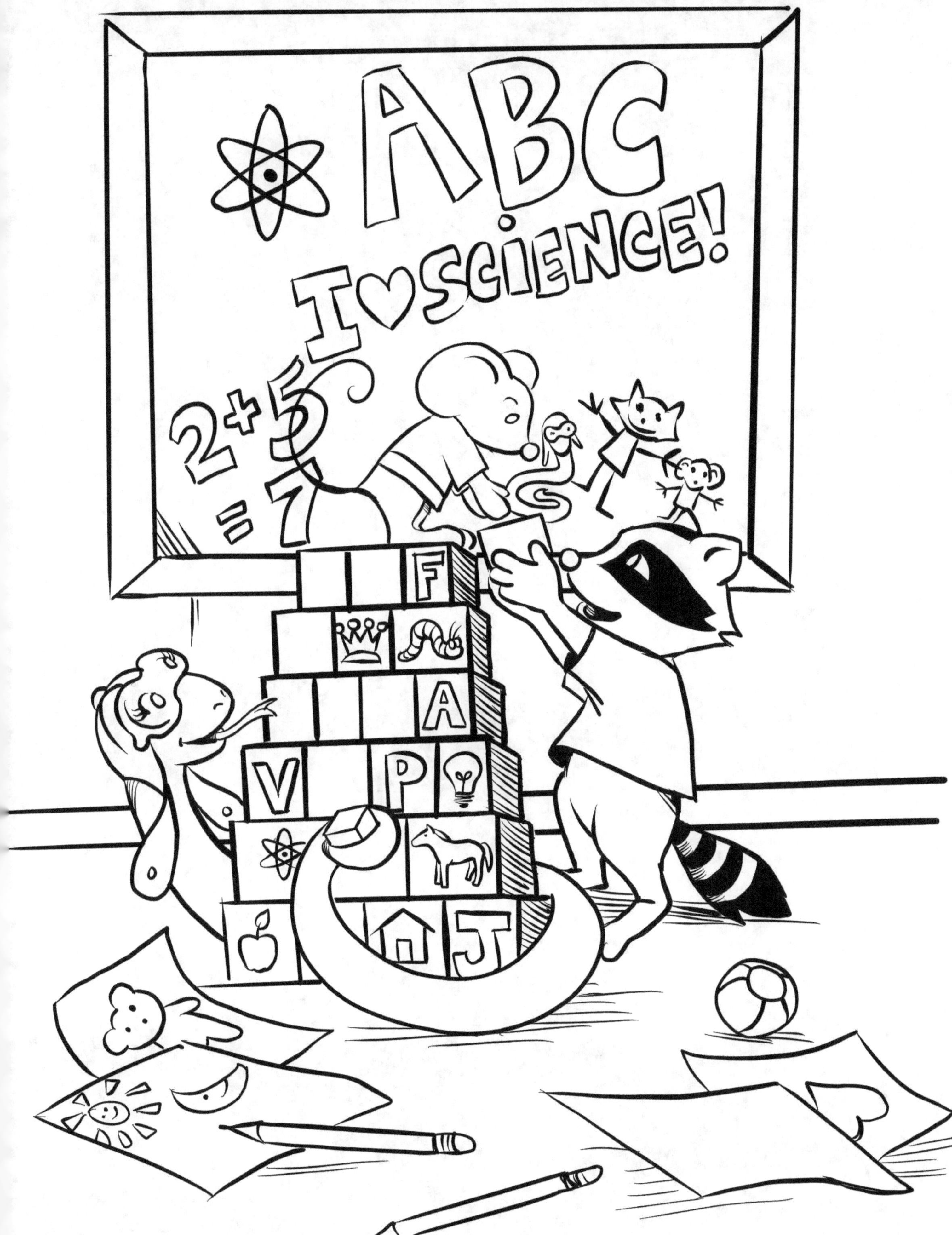
ABC
I ♥ SCIENCE!
2+5
=7
F
A
V
P
J

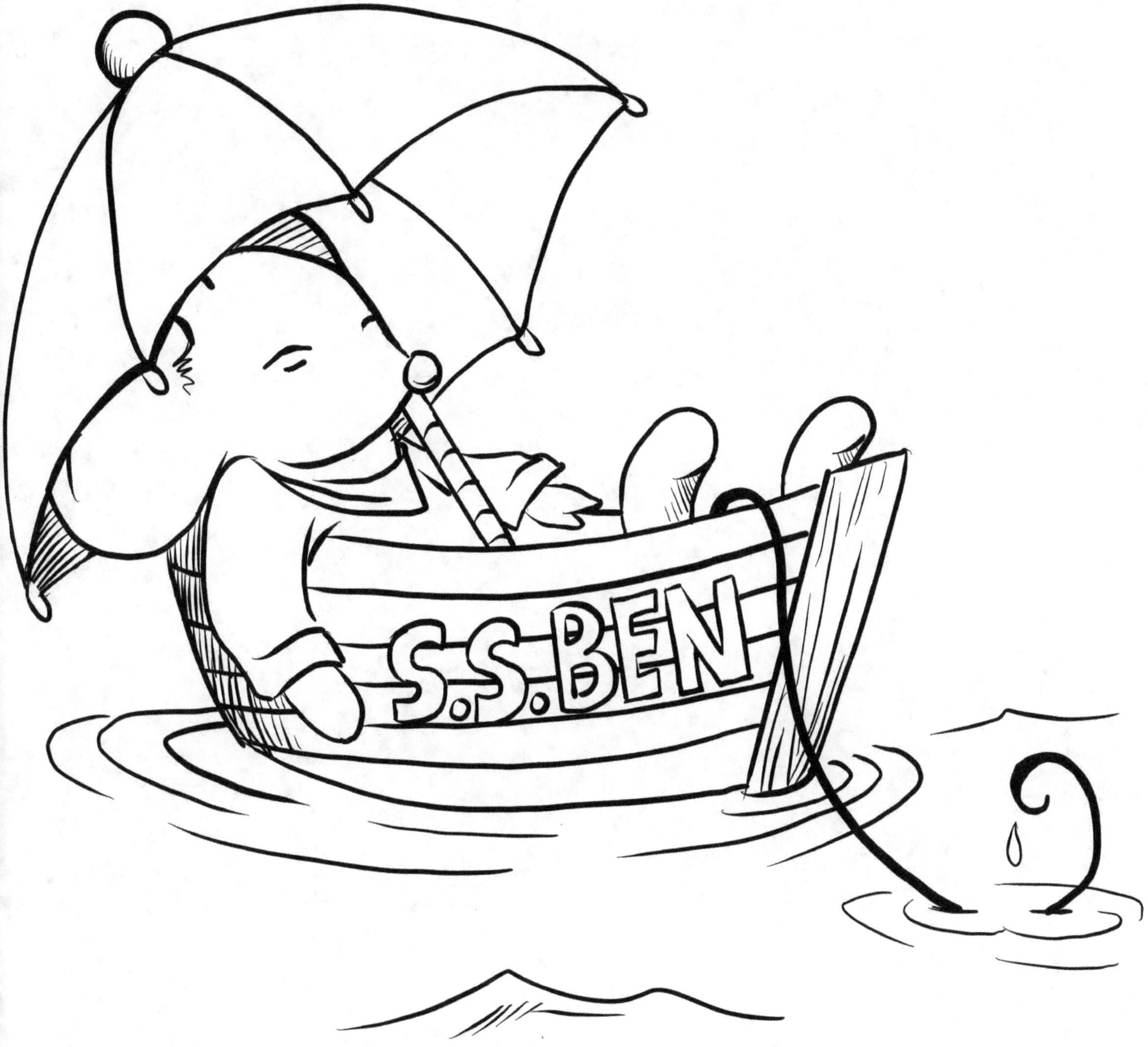
S.S.BEN

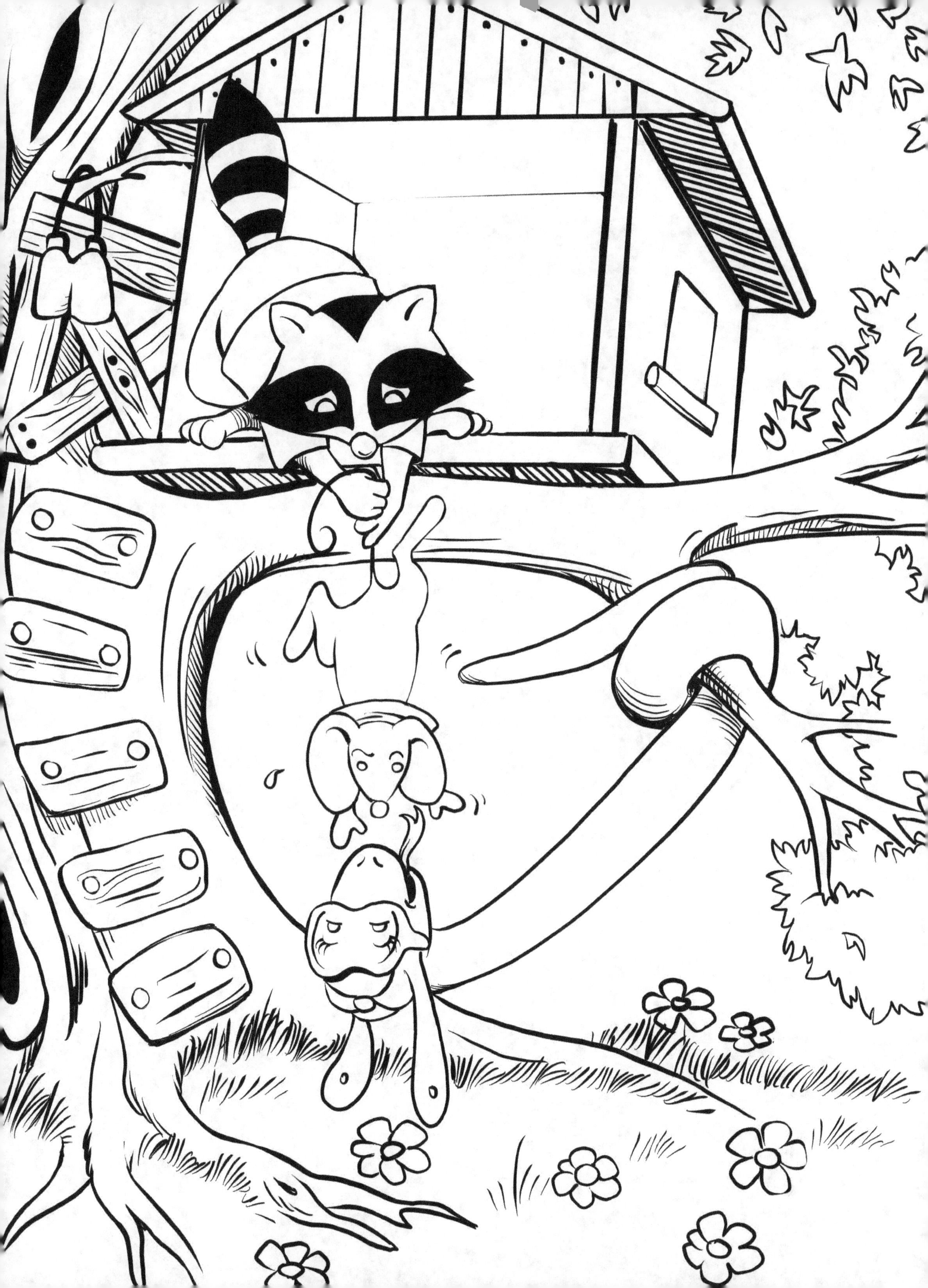

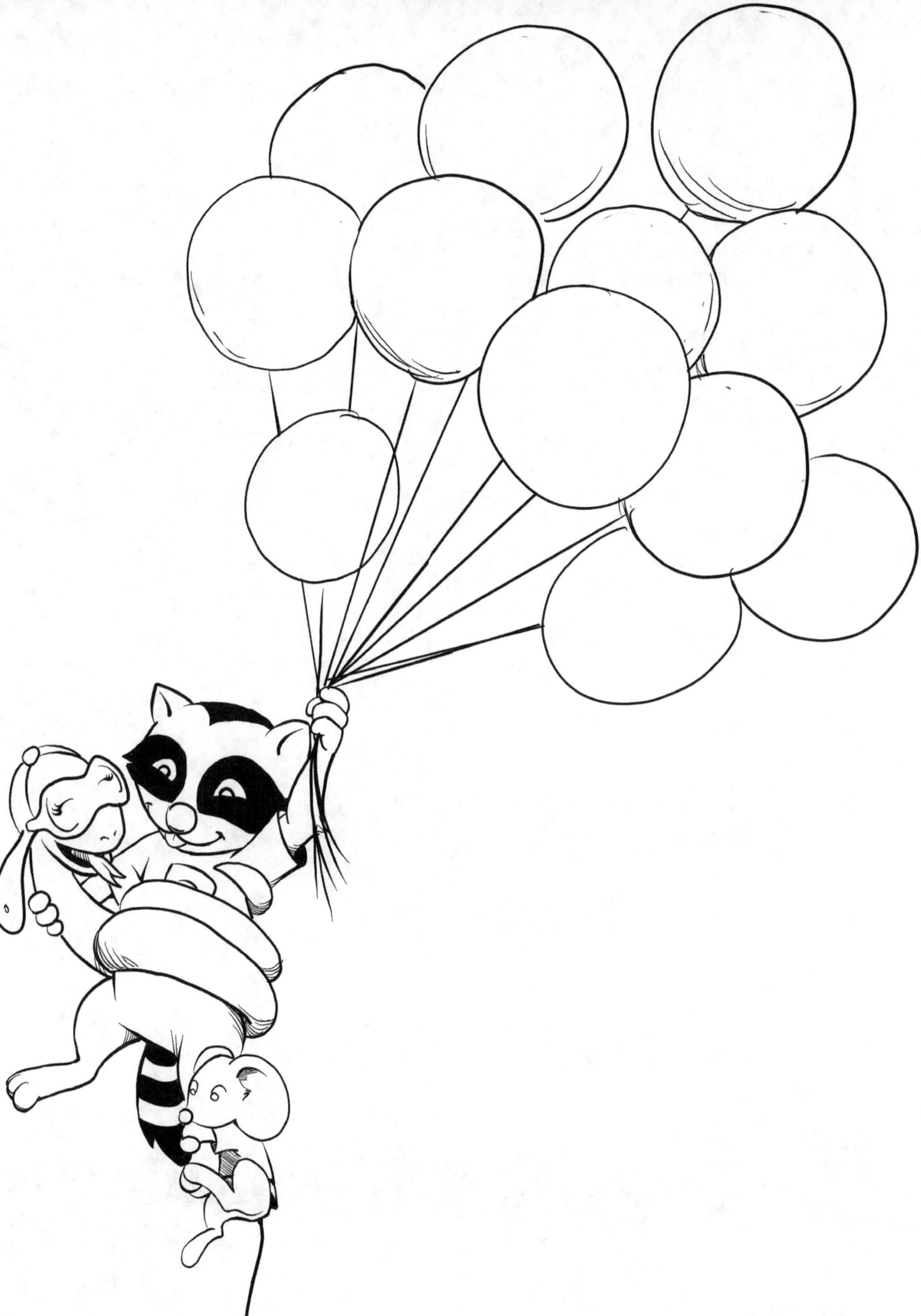

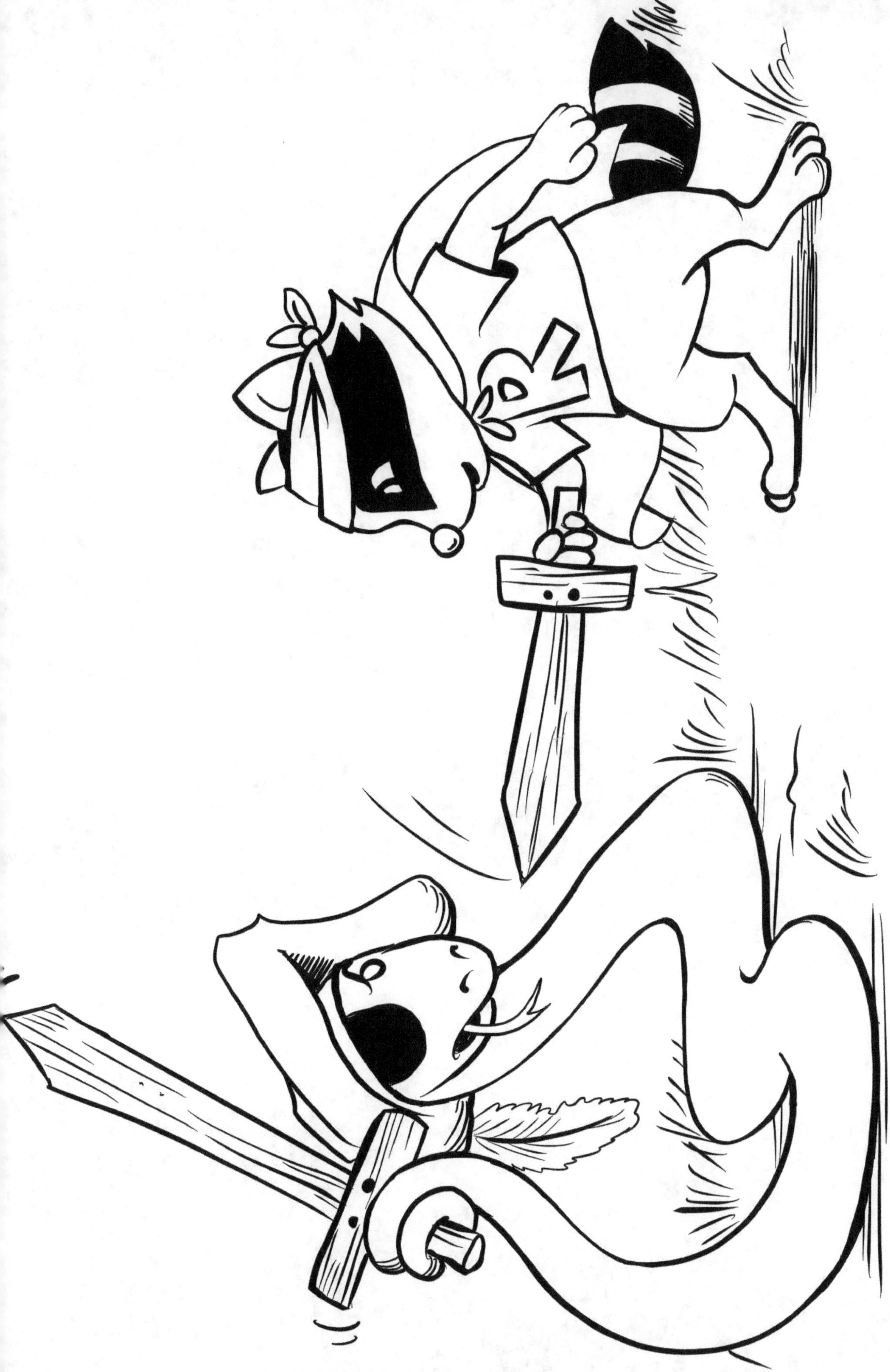

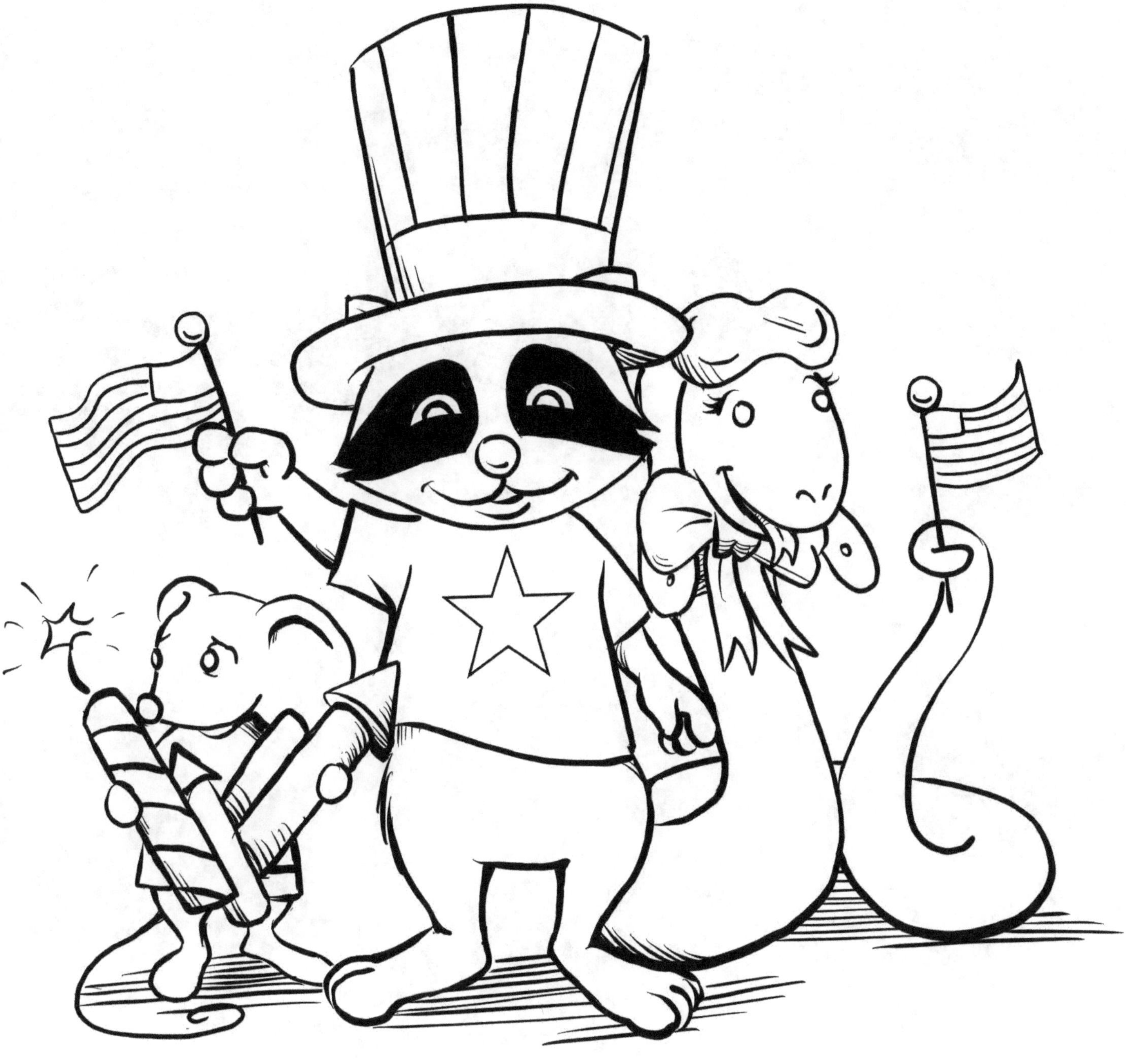

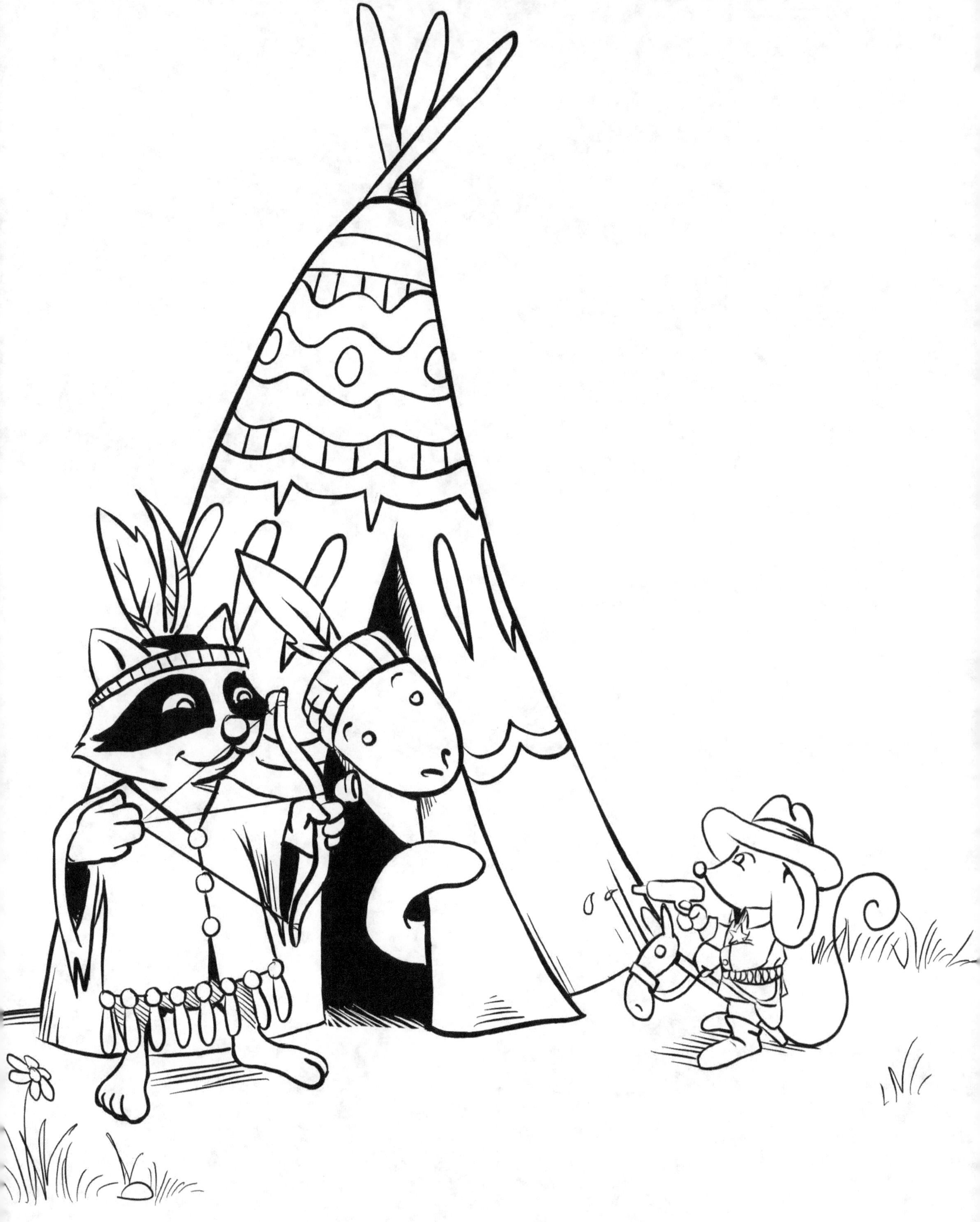

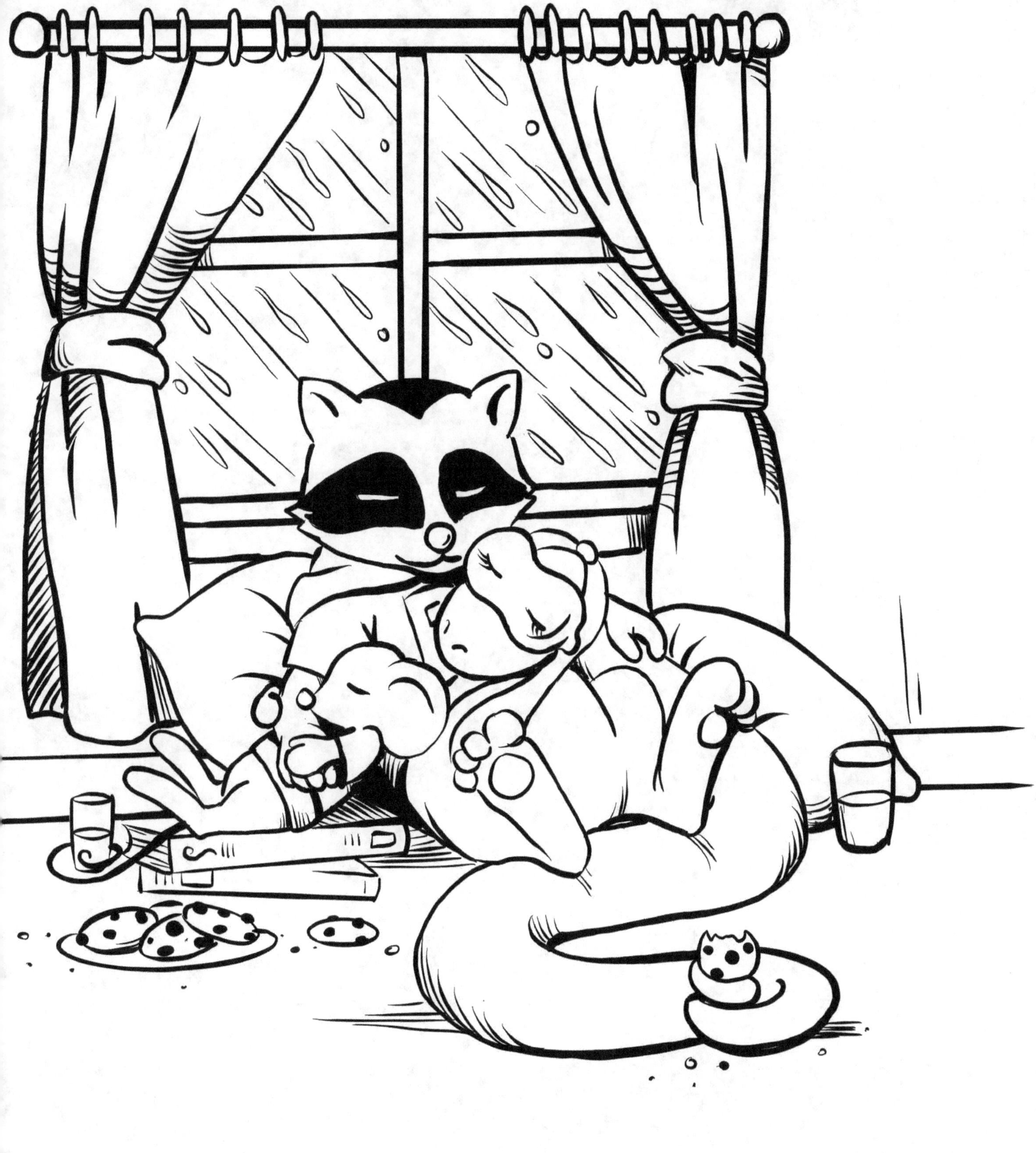

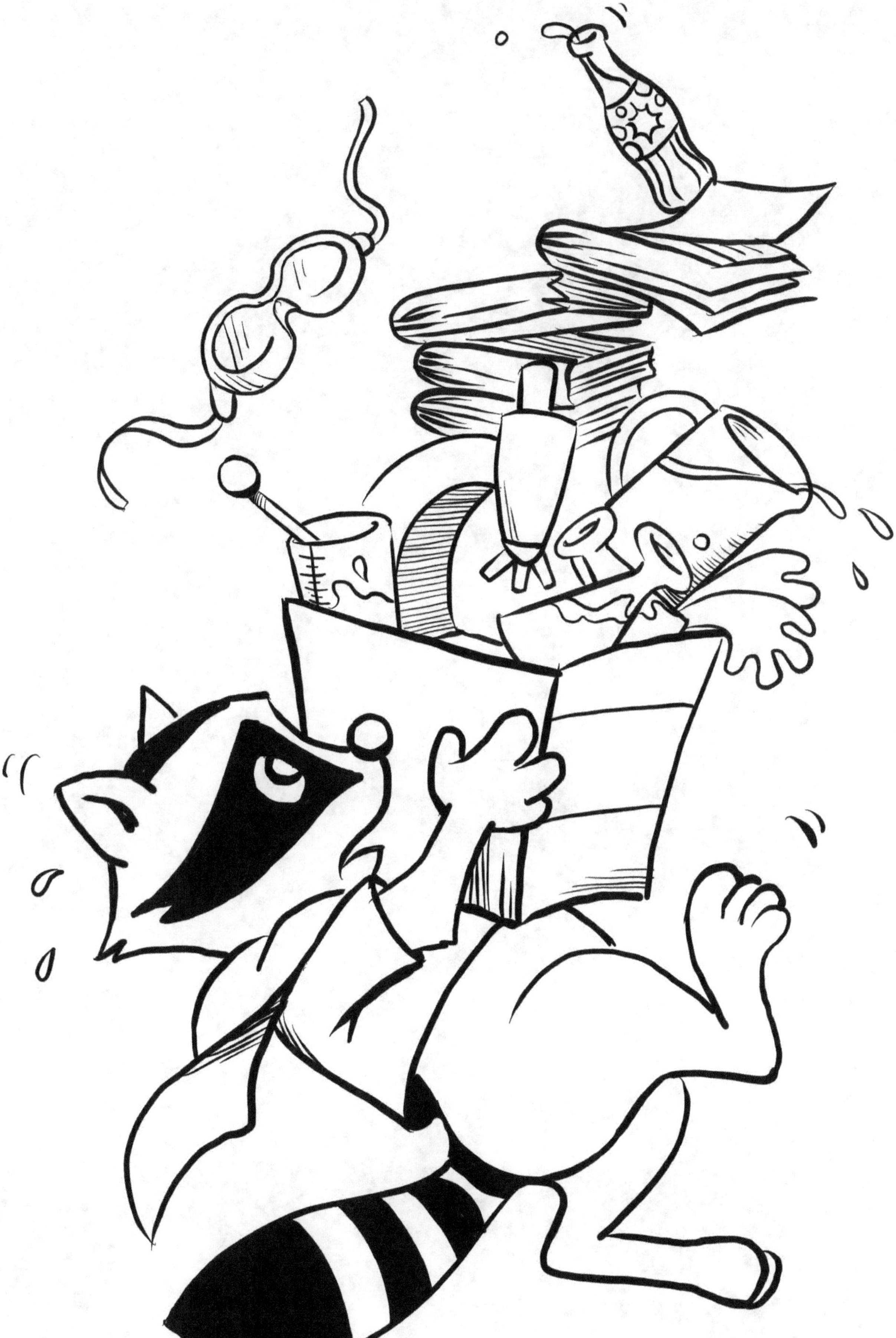

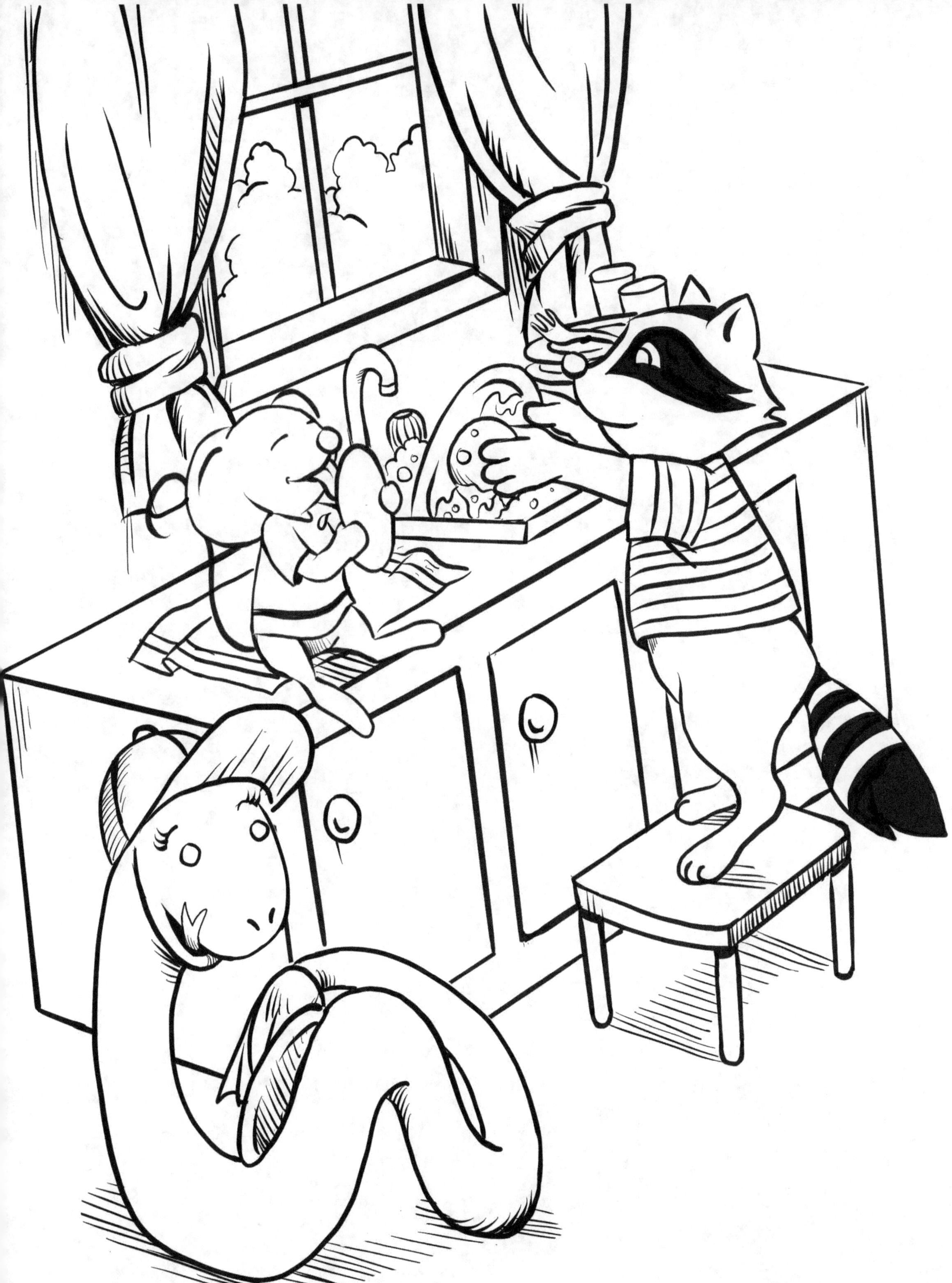

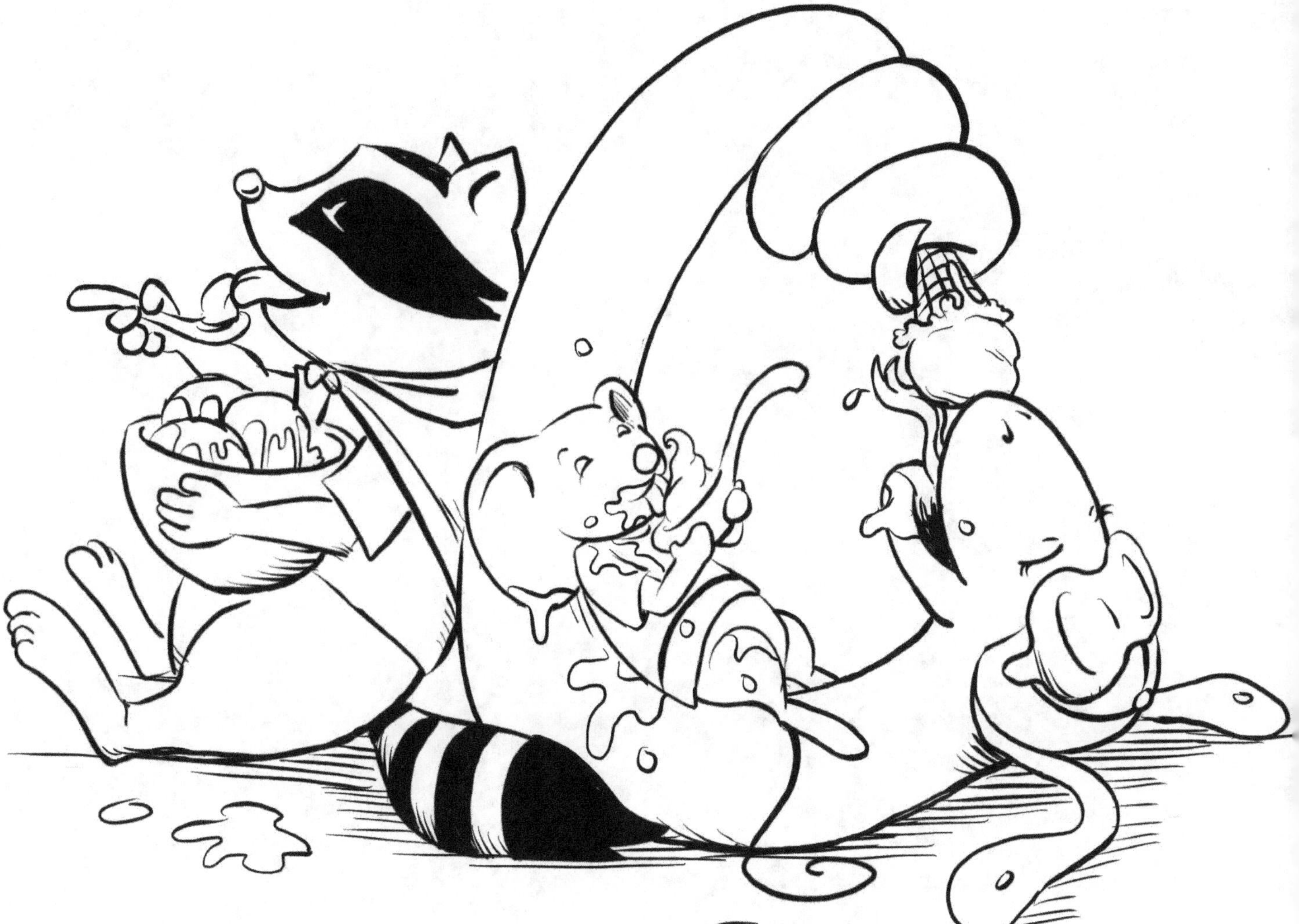

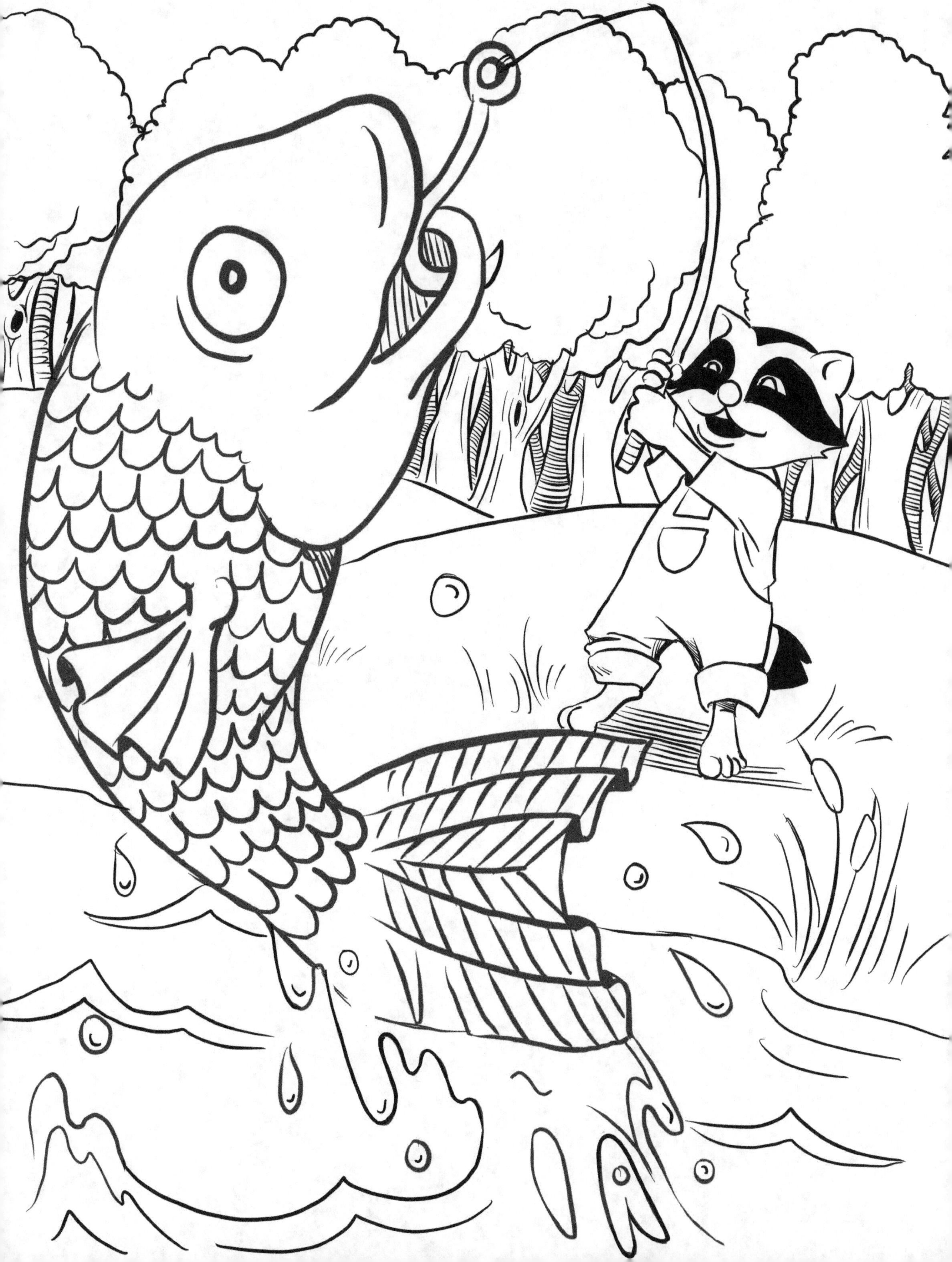

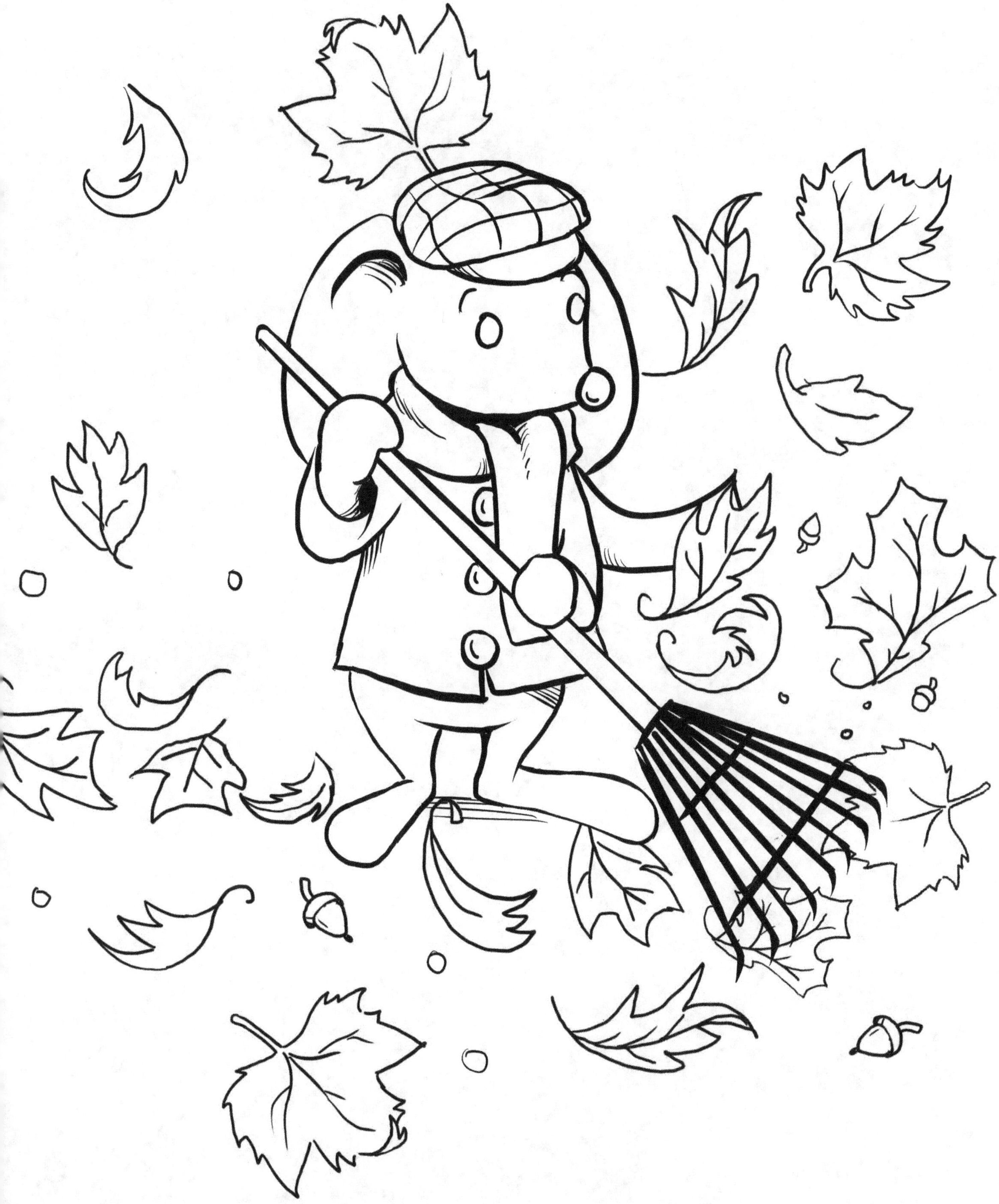

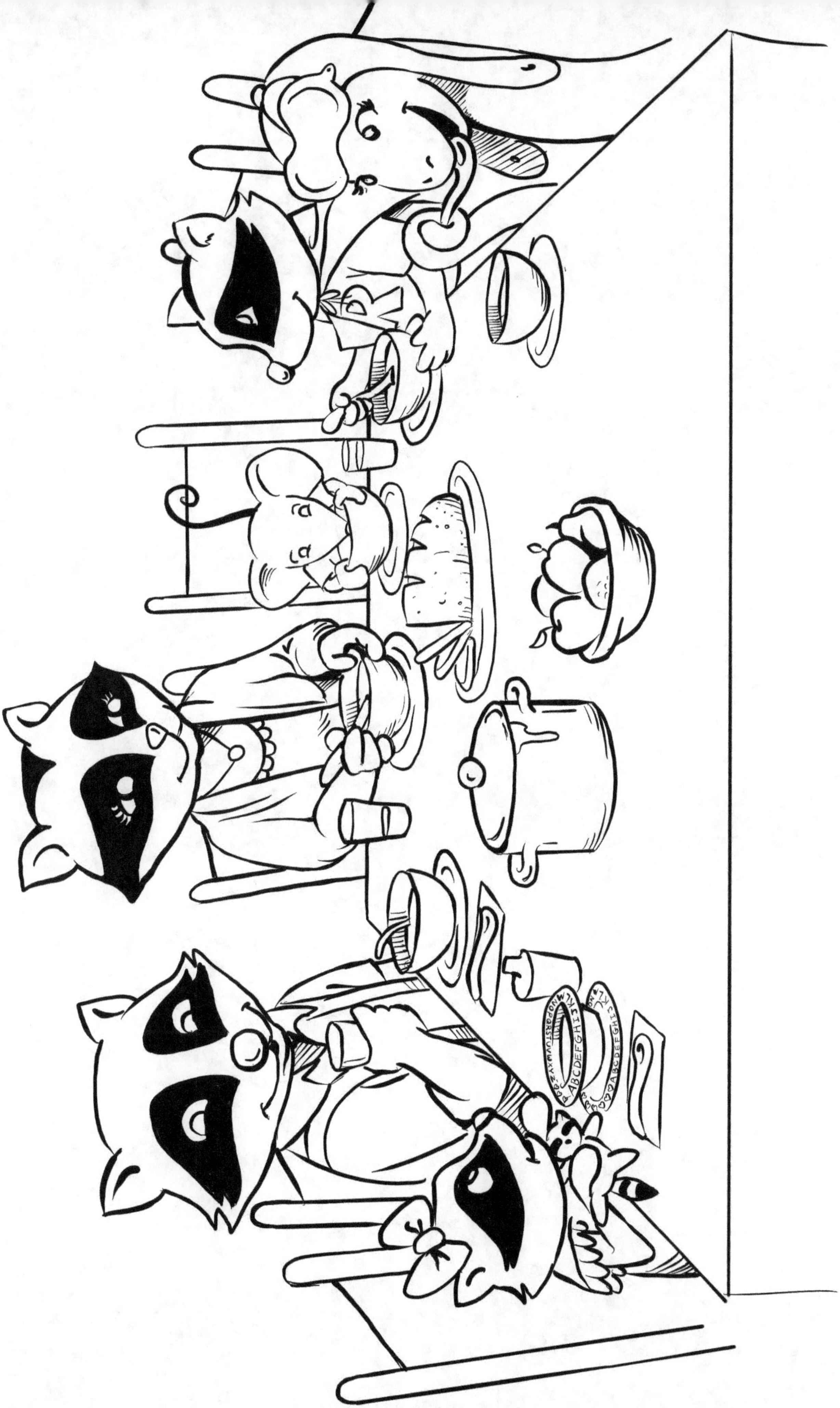

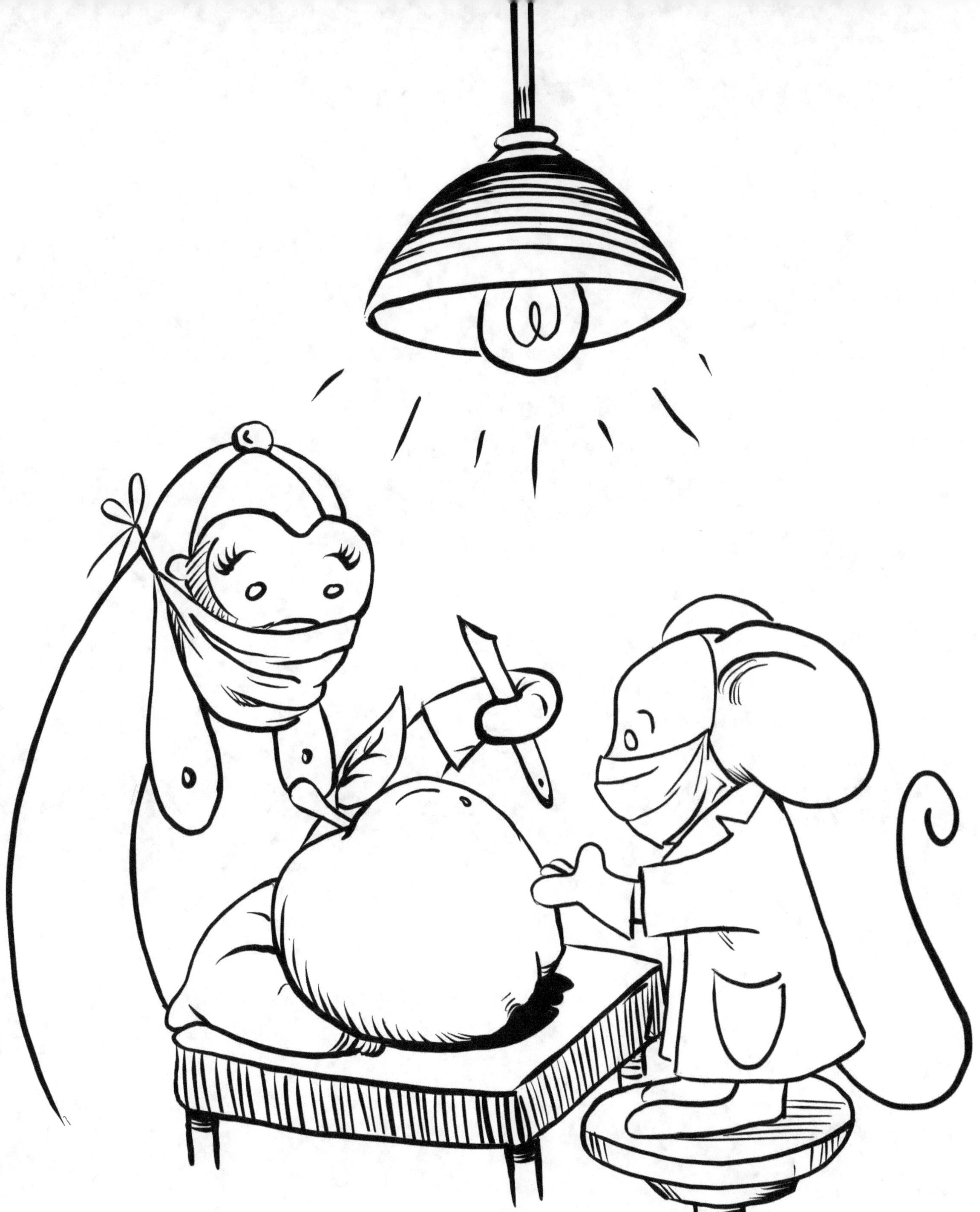

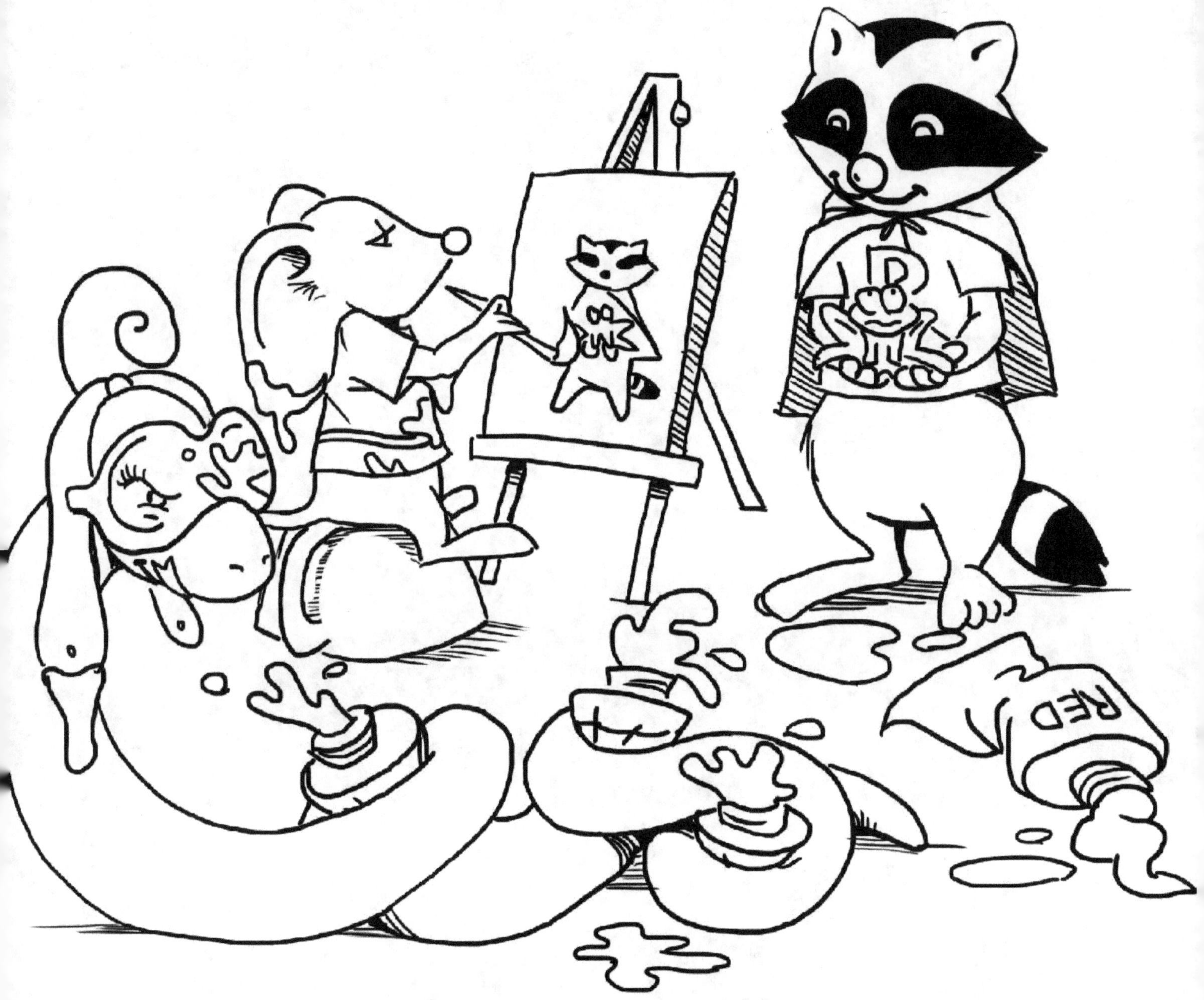
R
RED

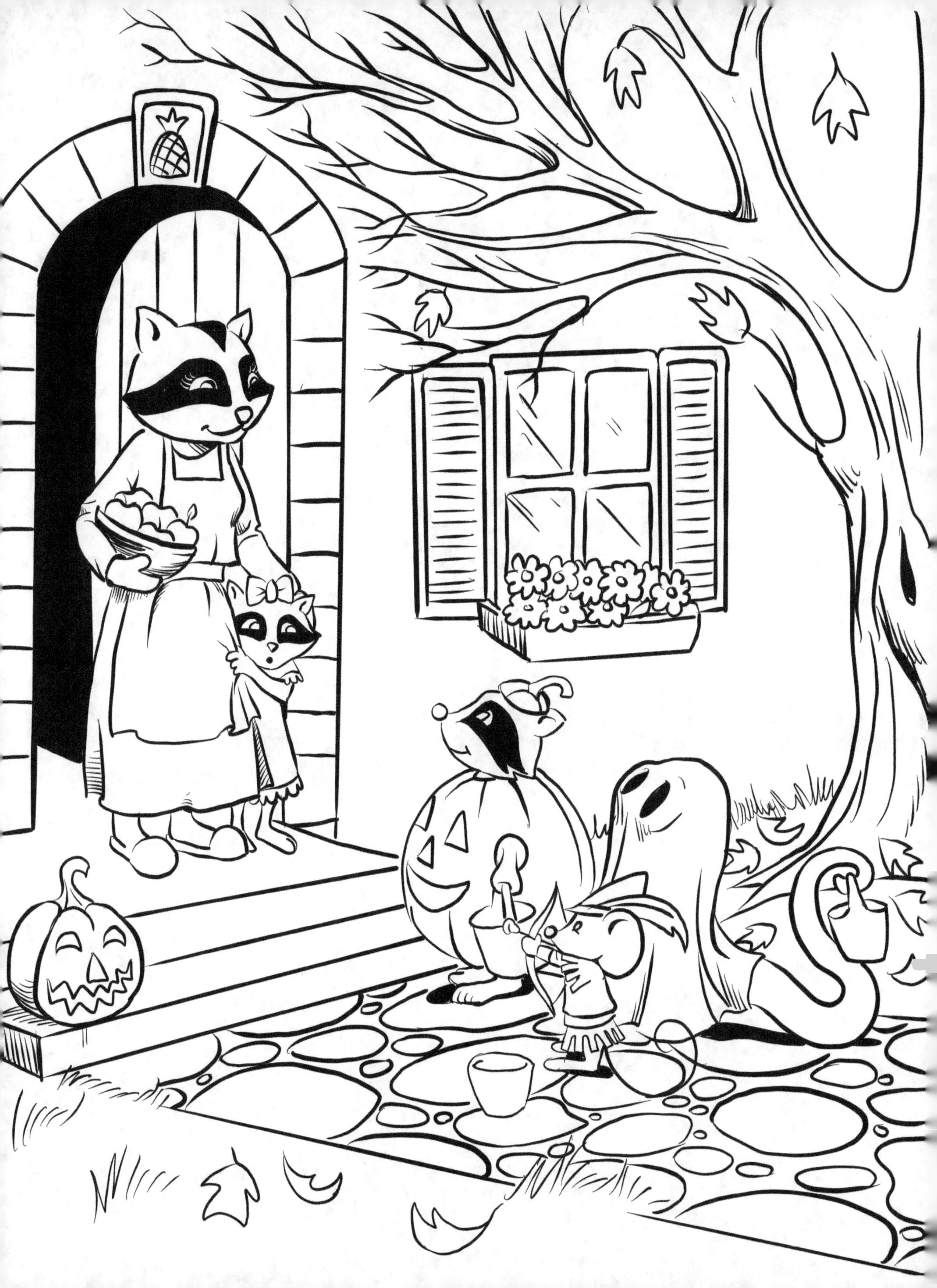

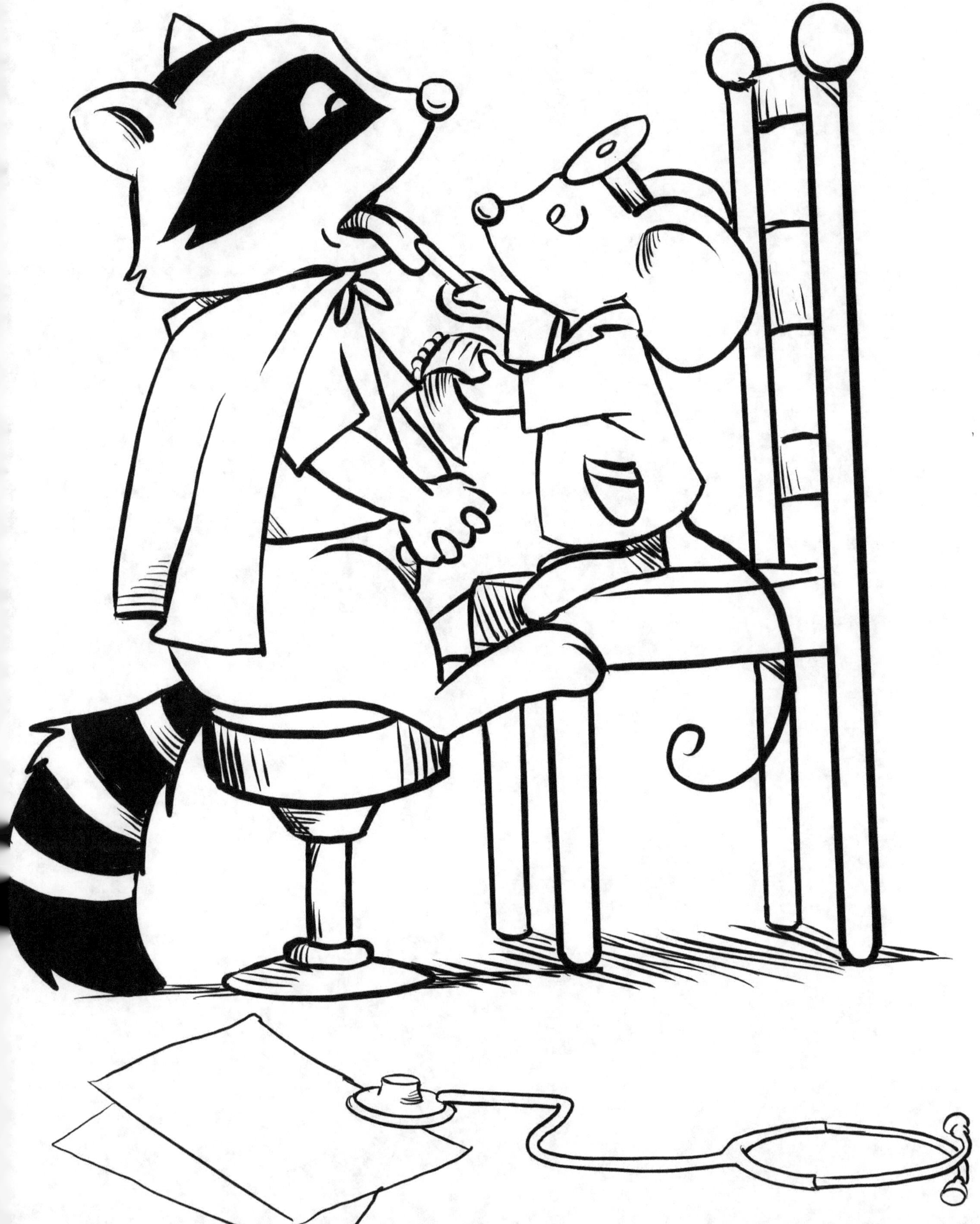

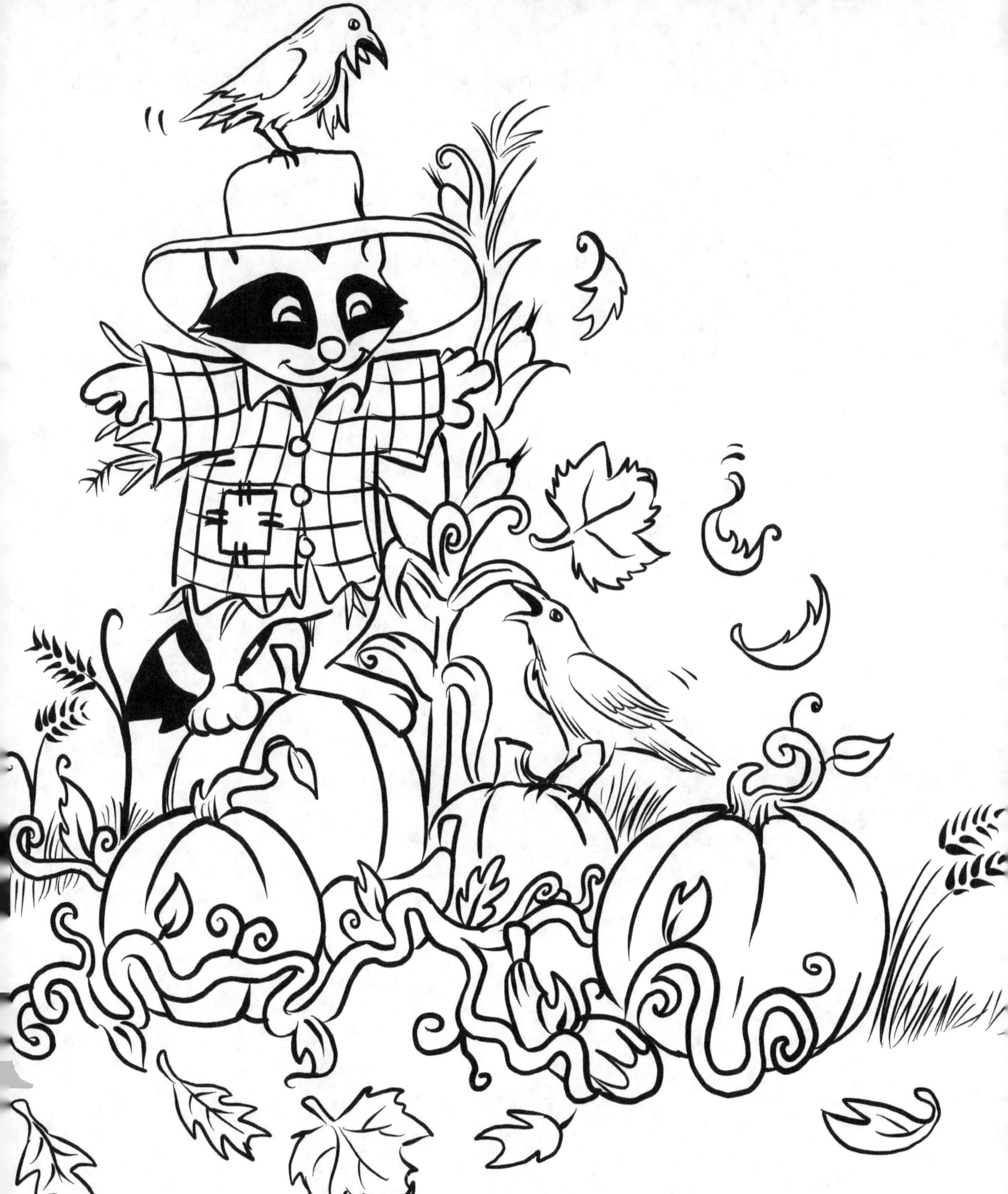

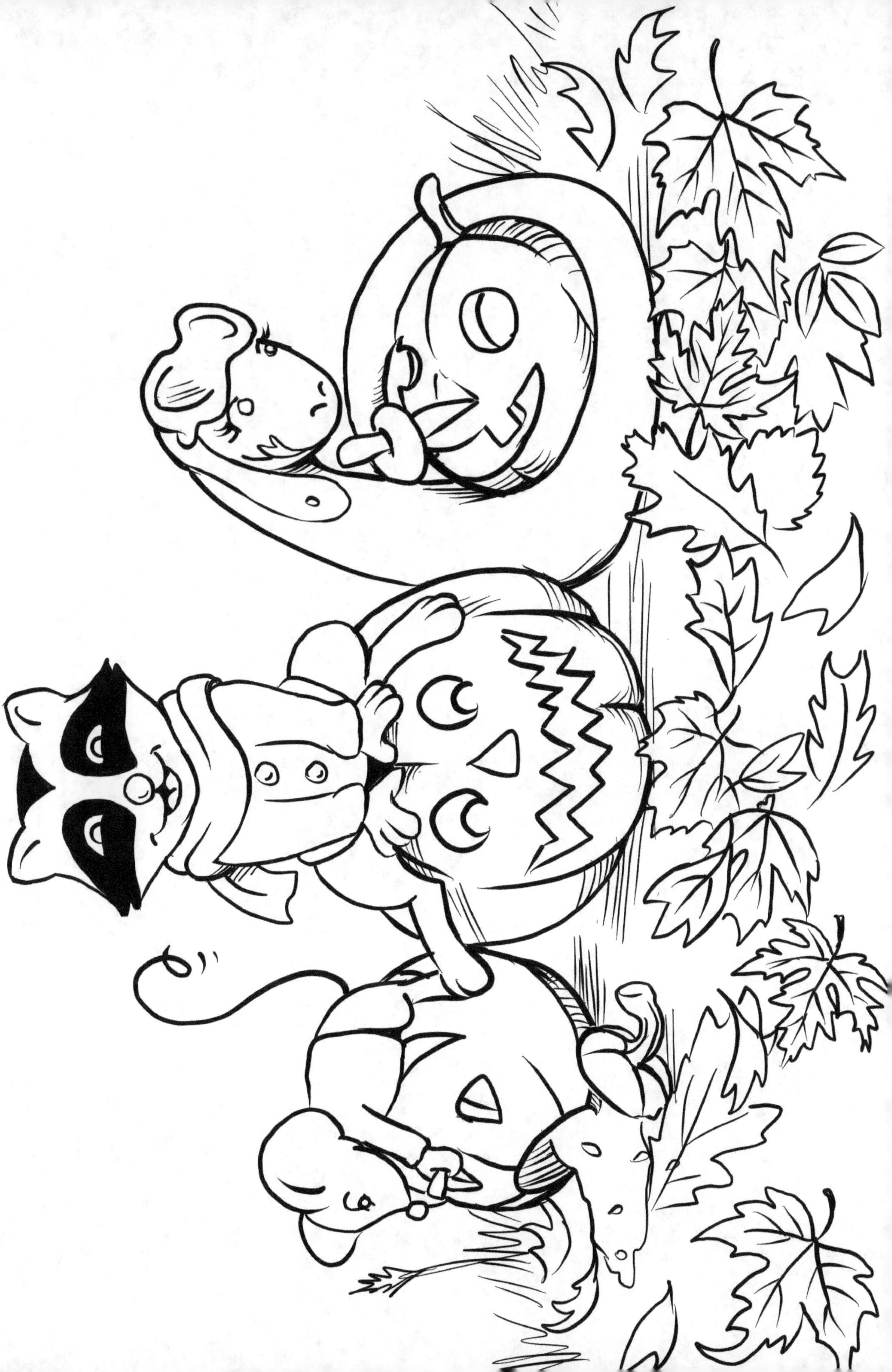

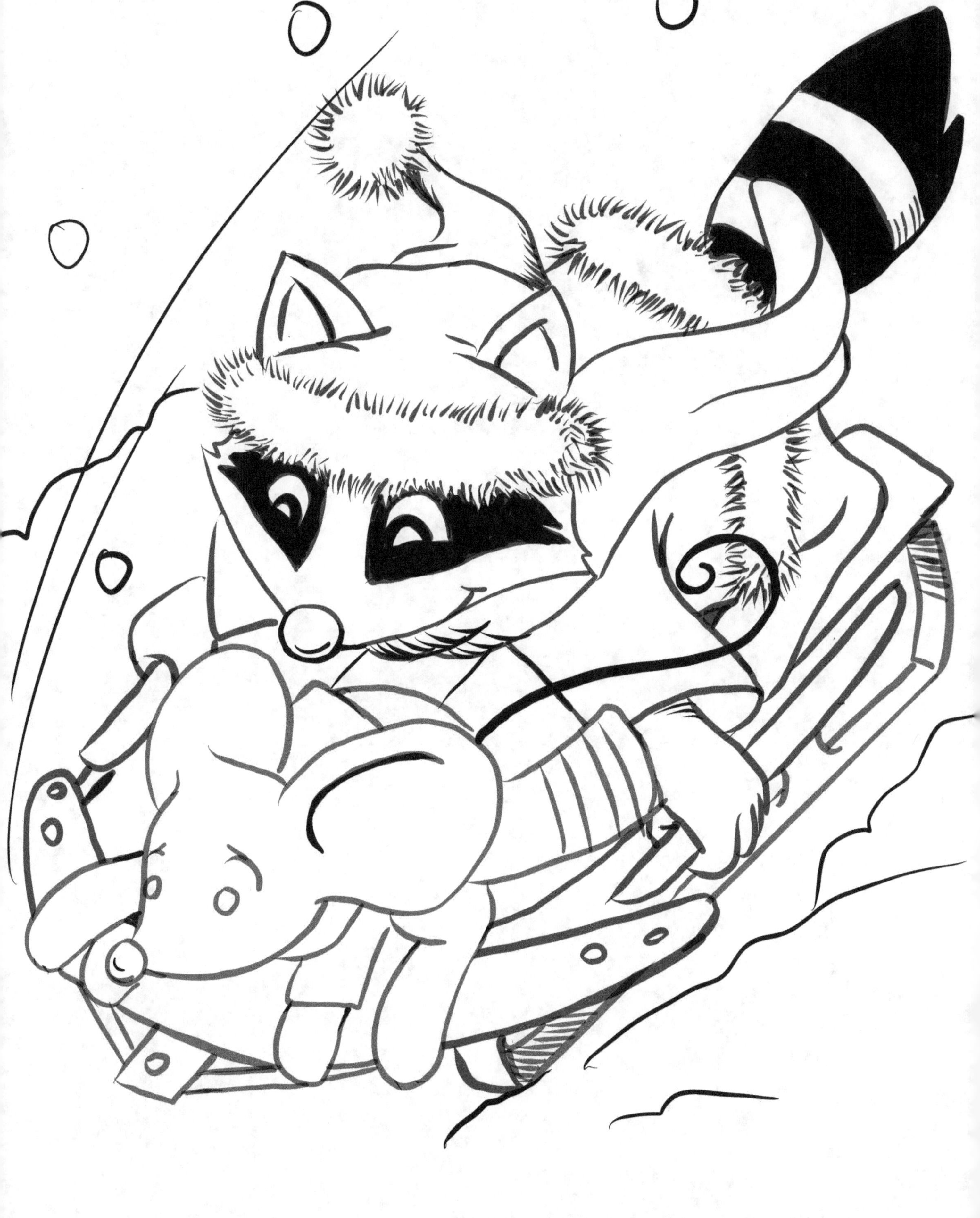

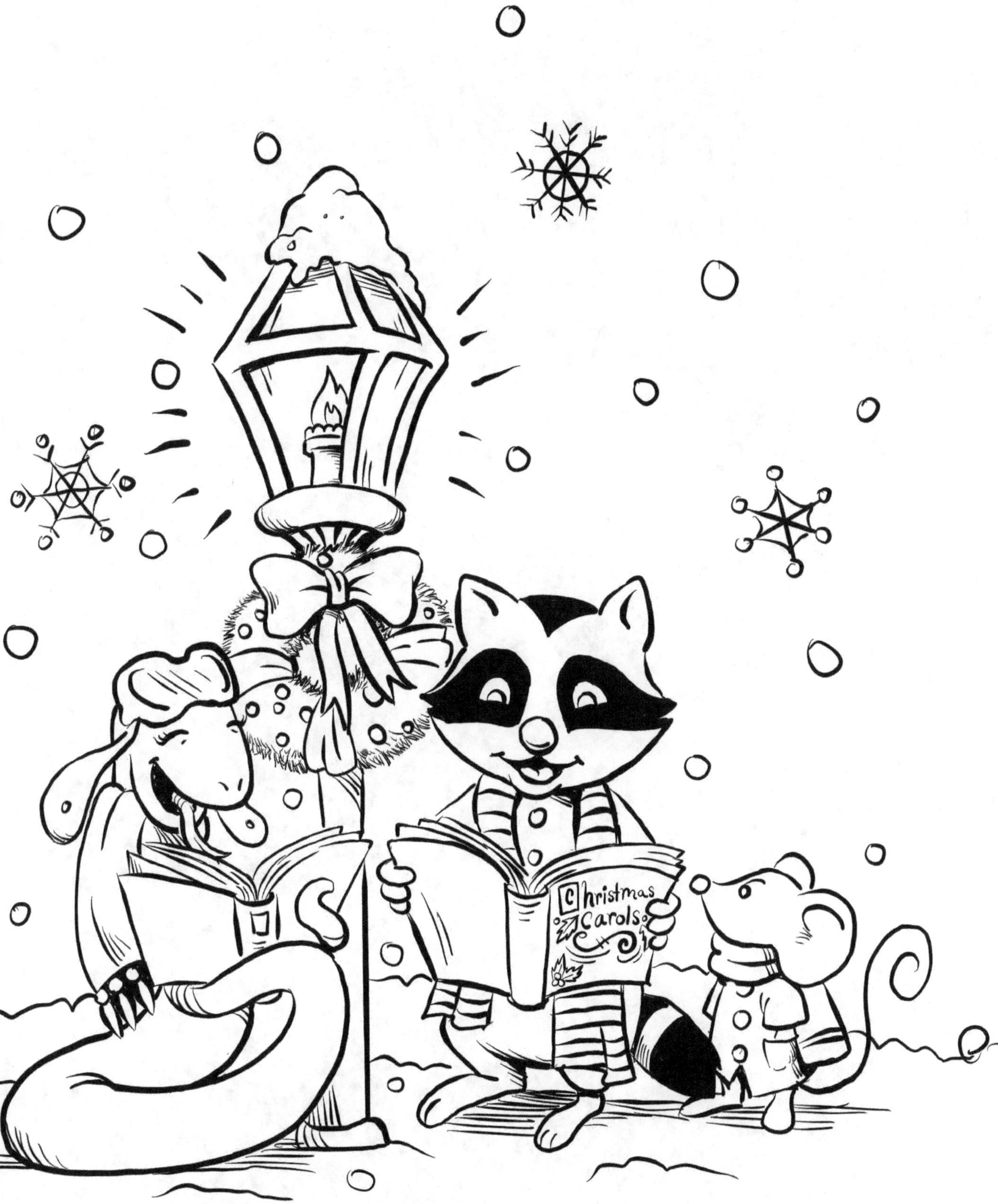
Christmas
Carols

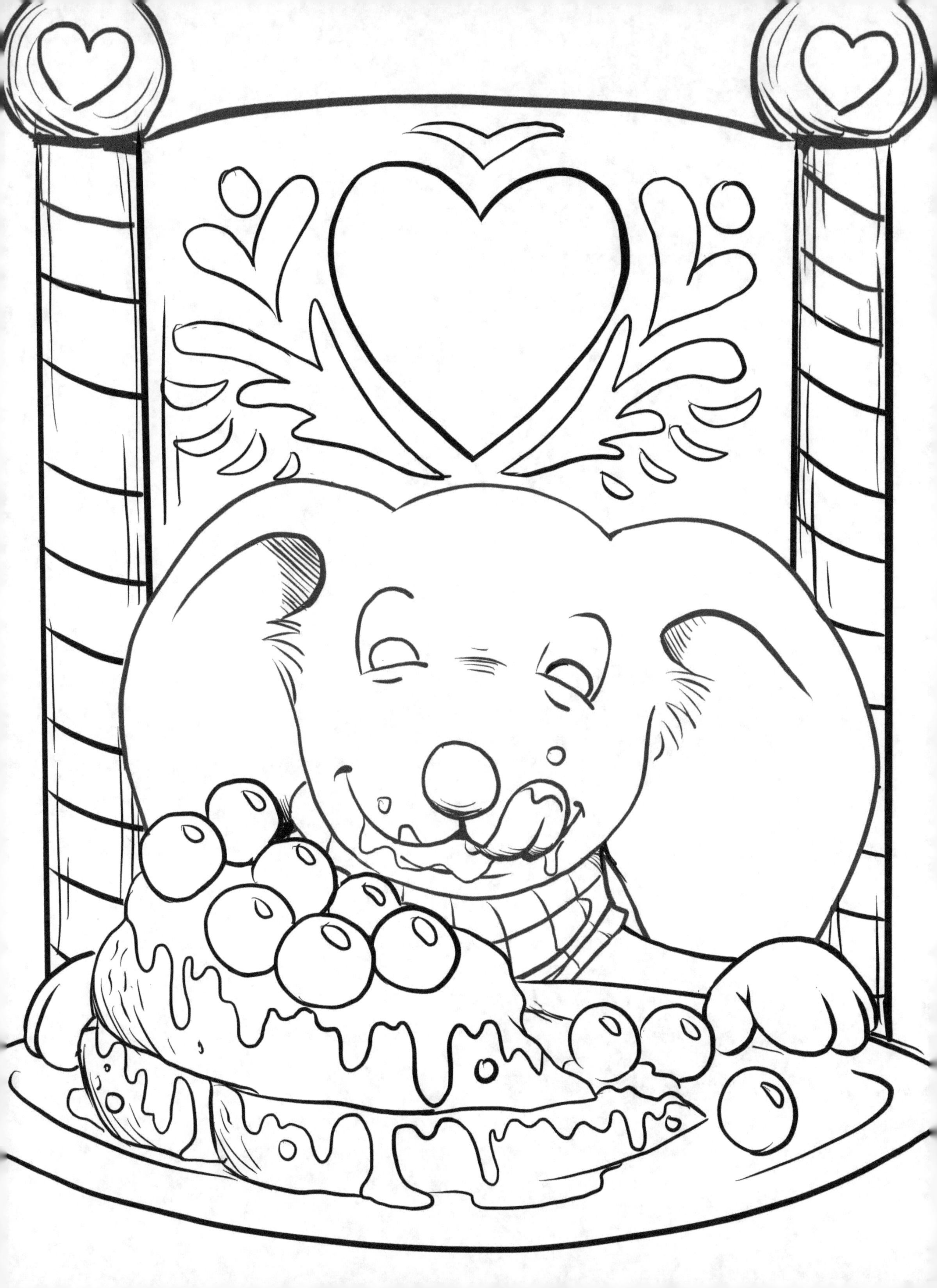

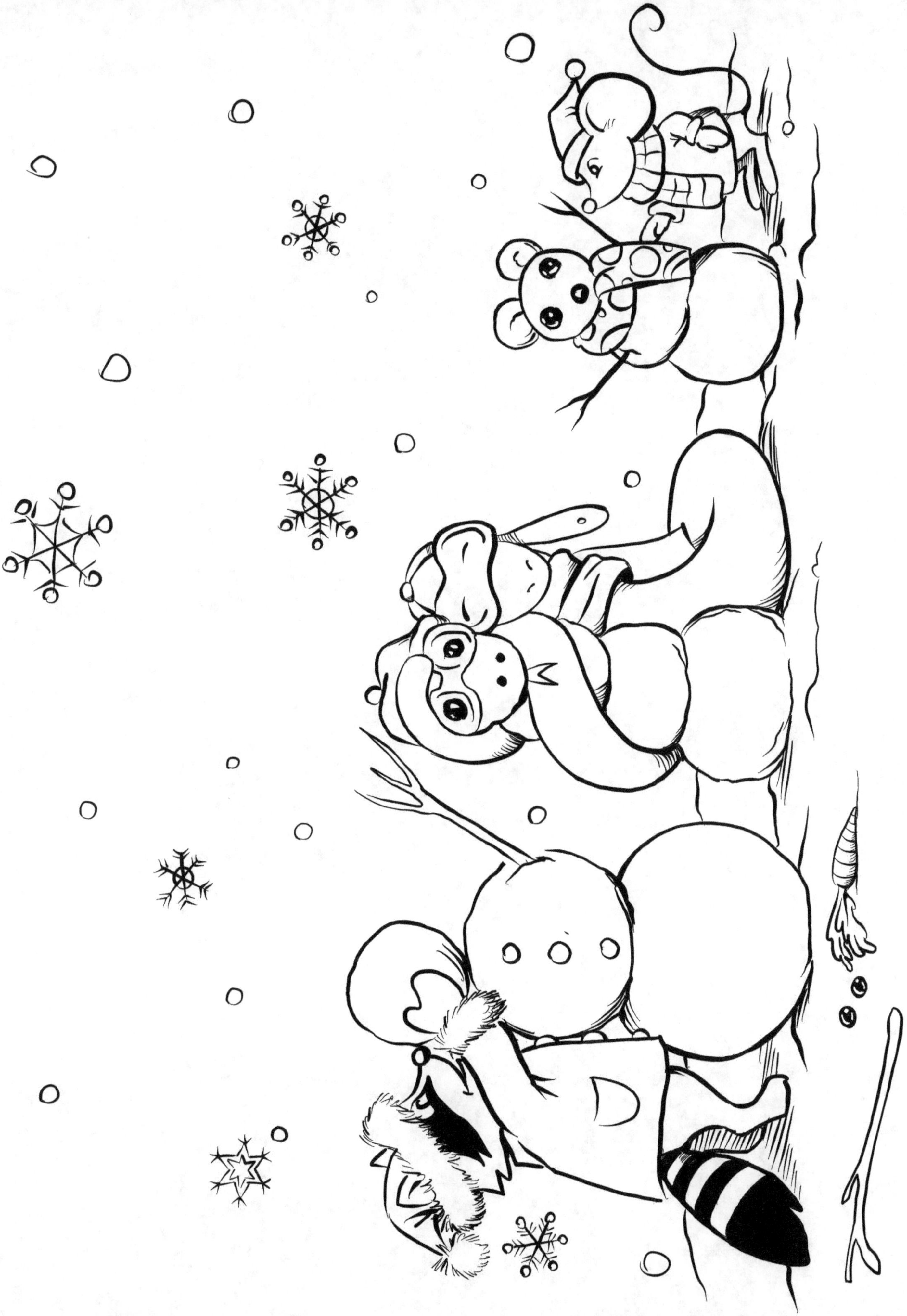

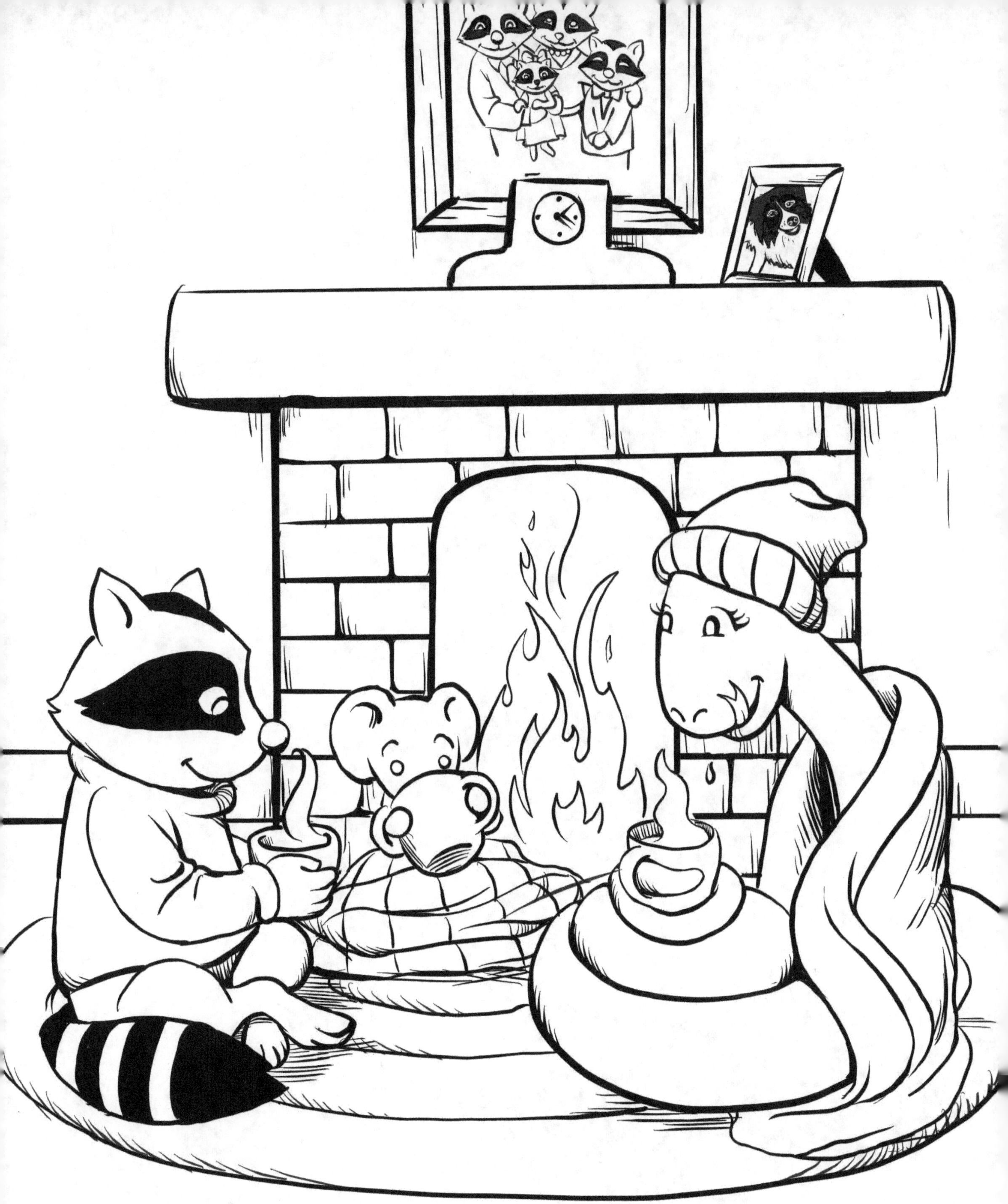

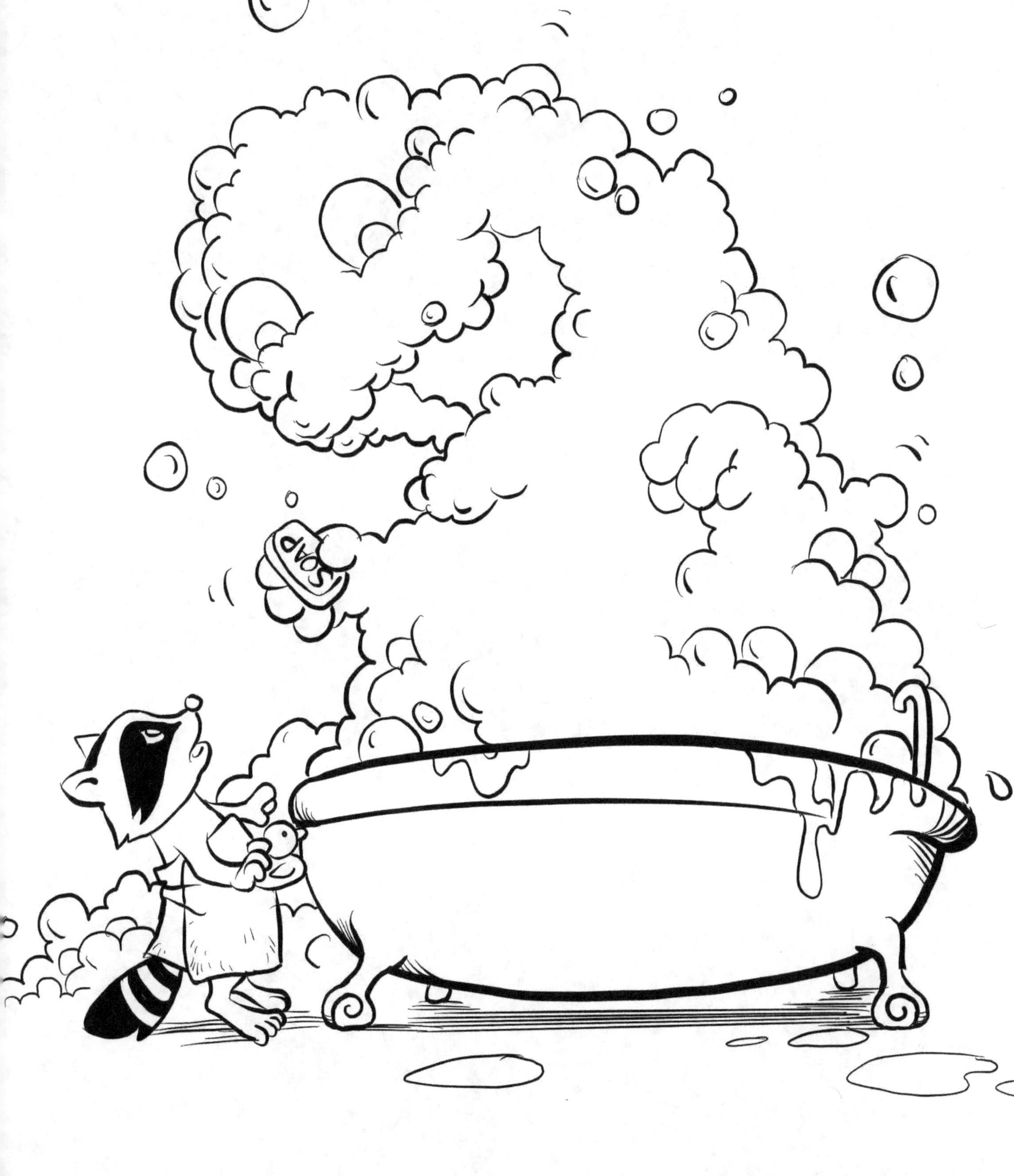
SOAP

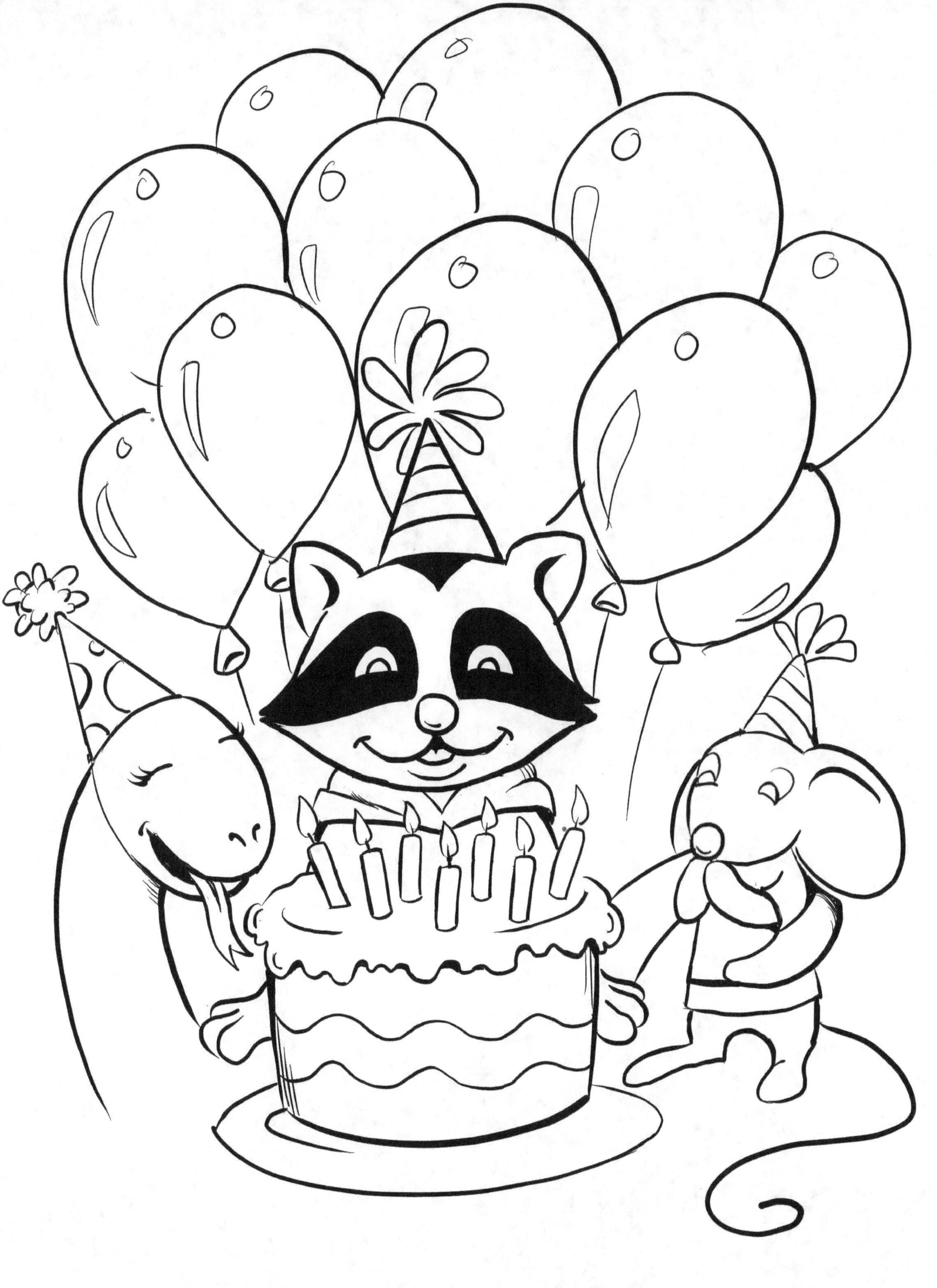

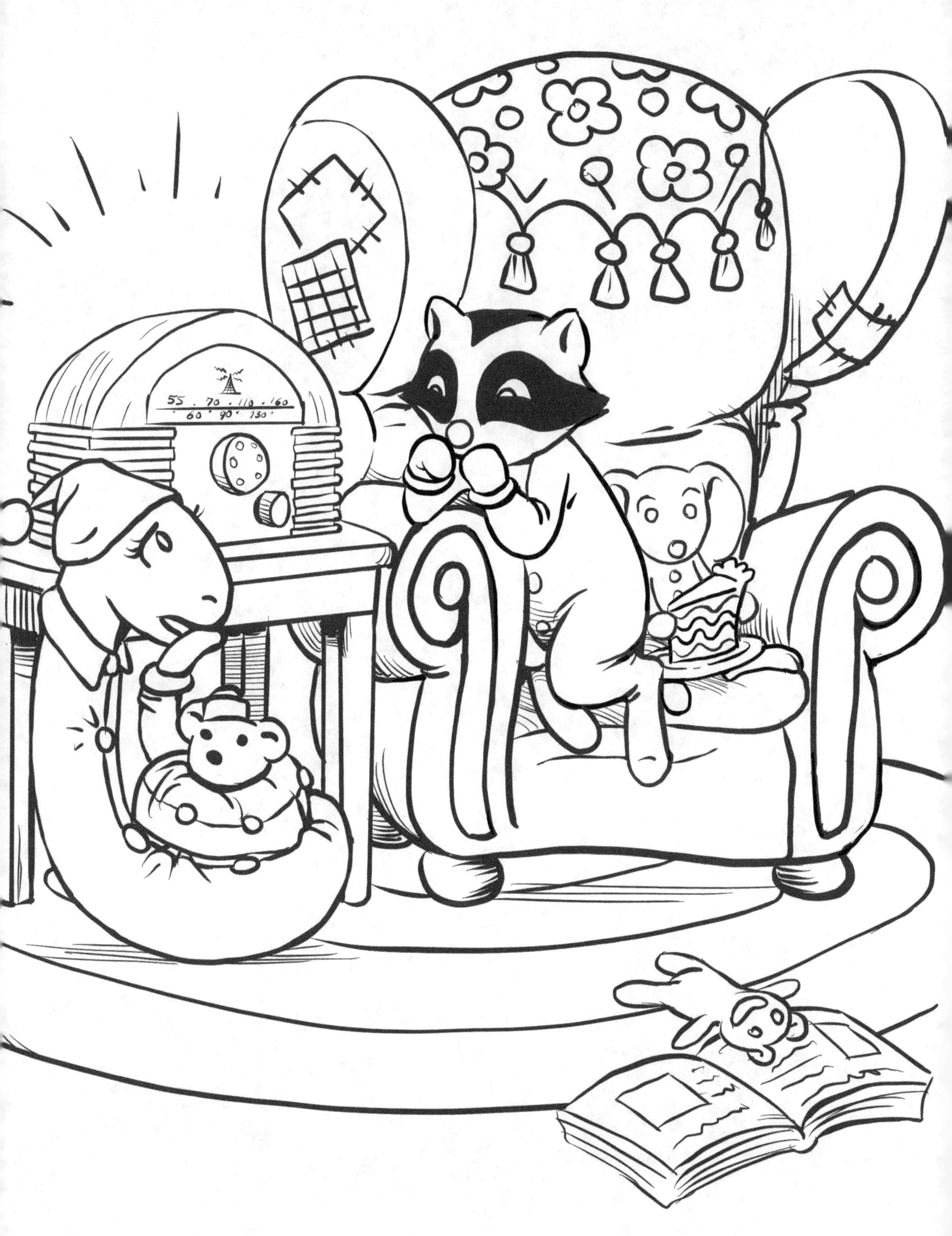
55 . 70 . 110 . 160
60 90 130

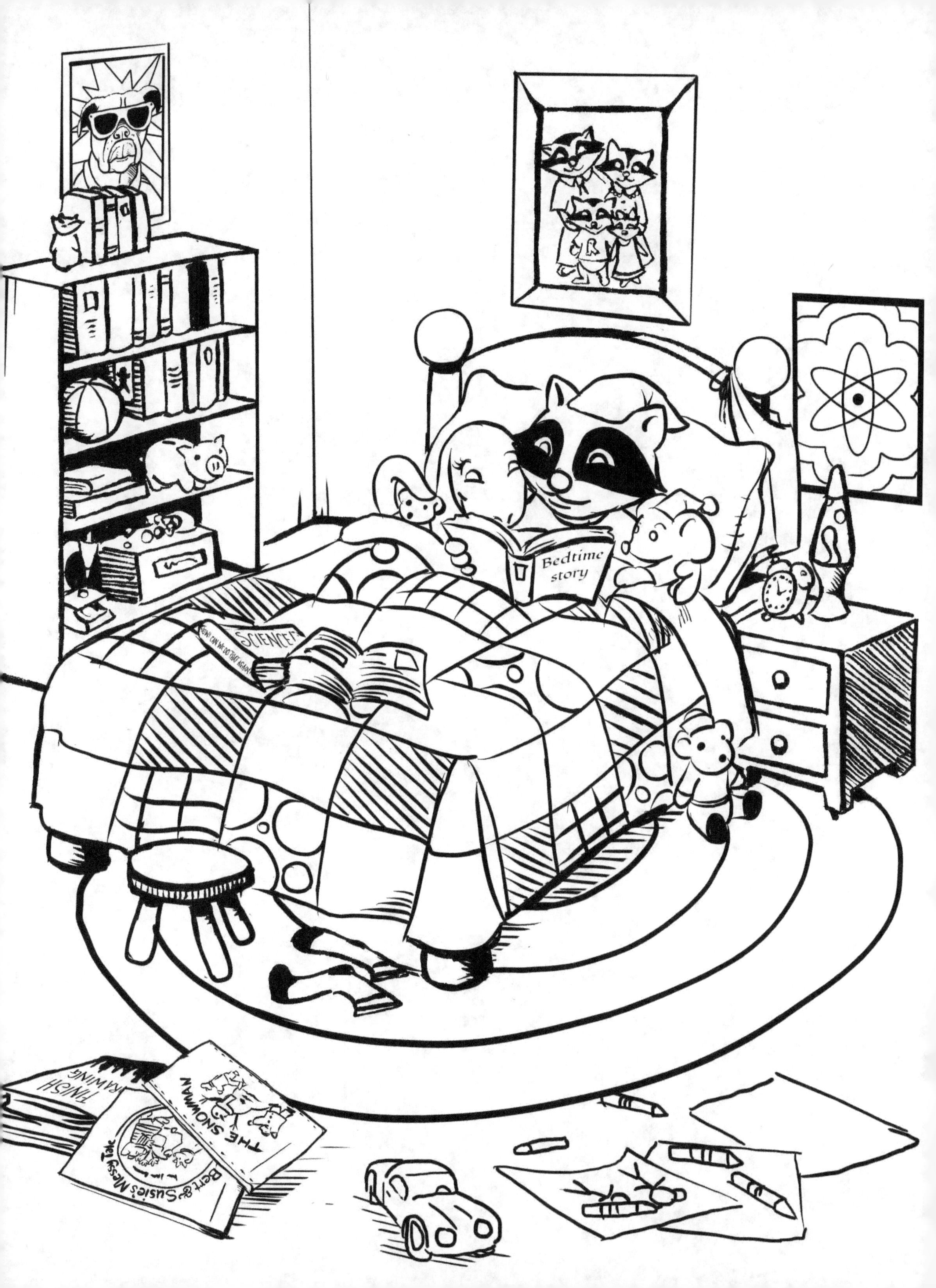
Bedtime story
SCIENCE!
WOW! CAN WE DO THAT AGAIN?
FINISH
RAWING
THE SNOWMAN
Bert & Susie's Messy Tale

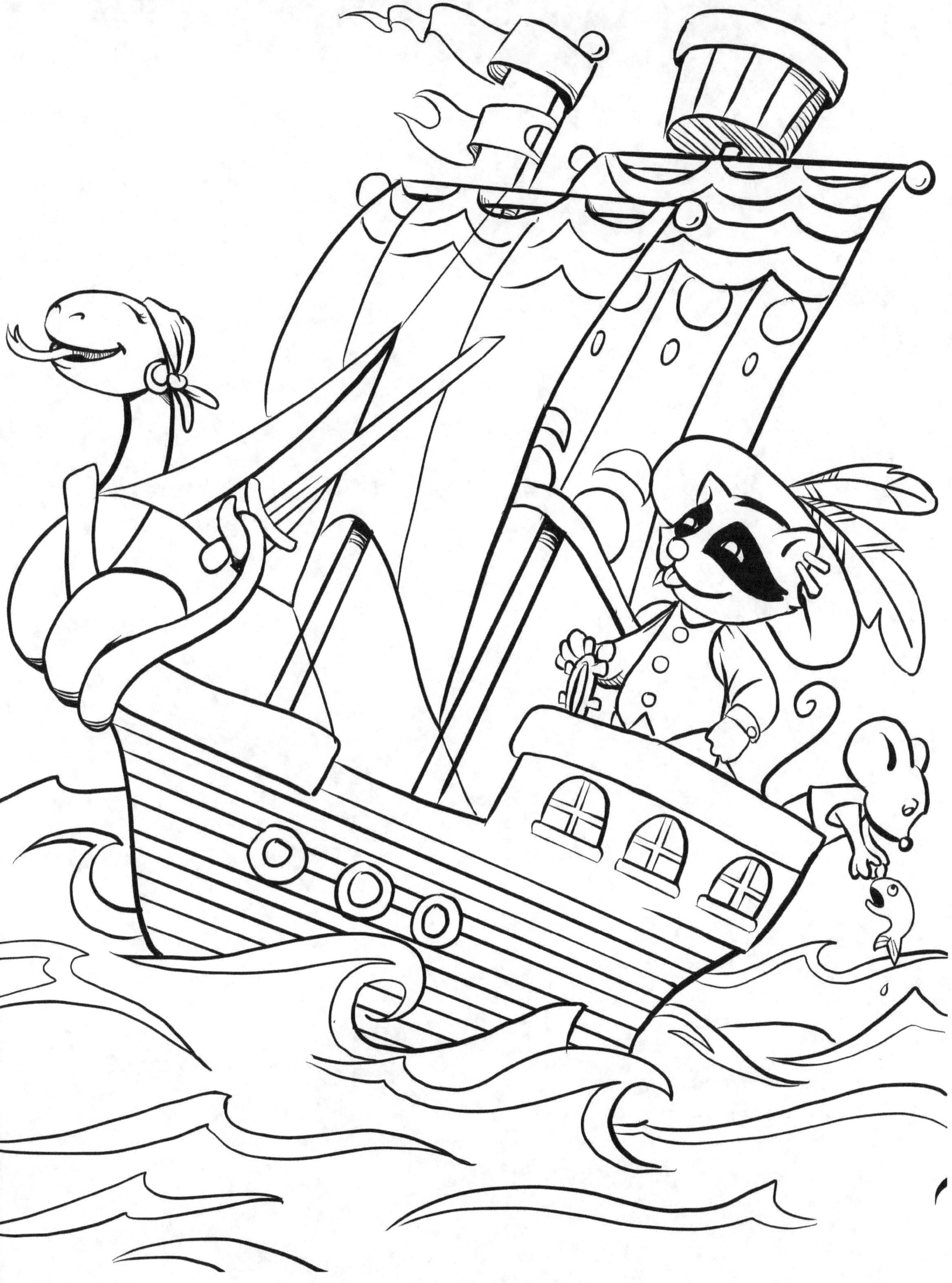

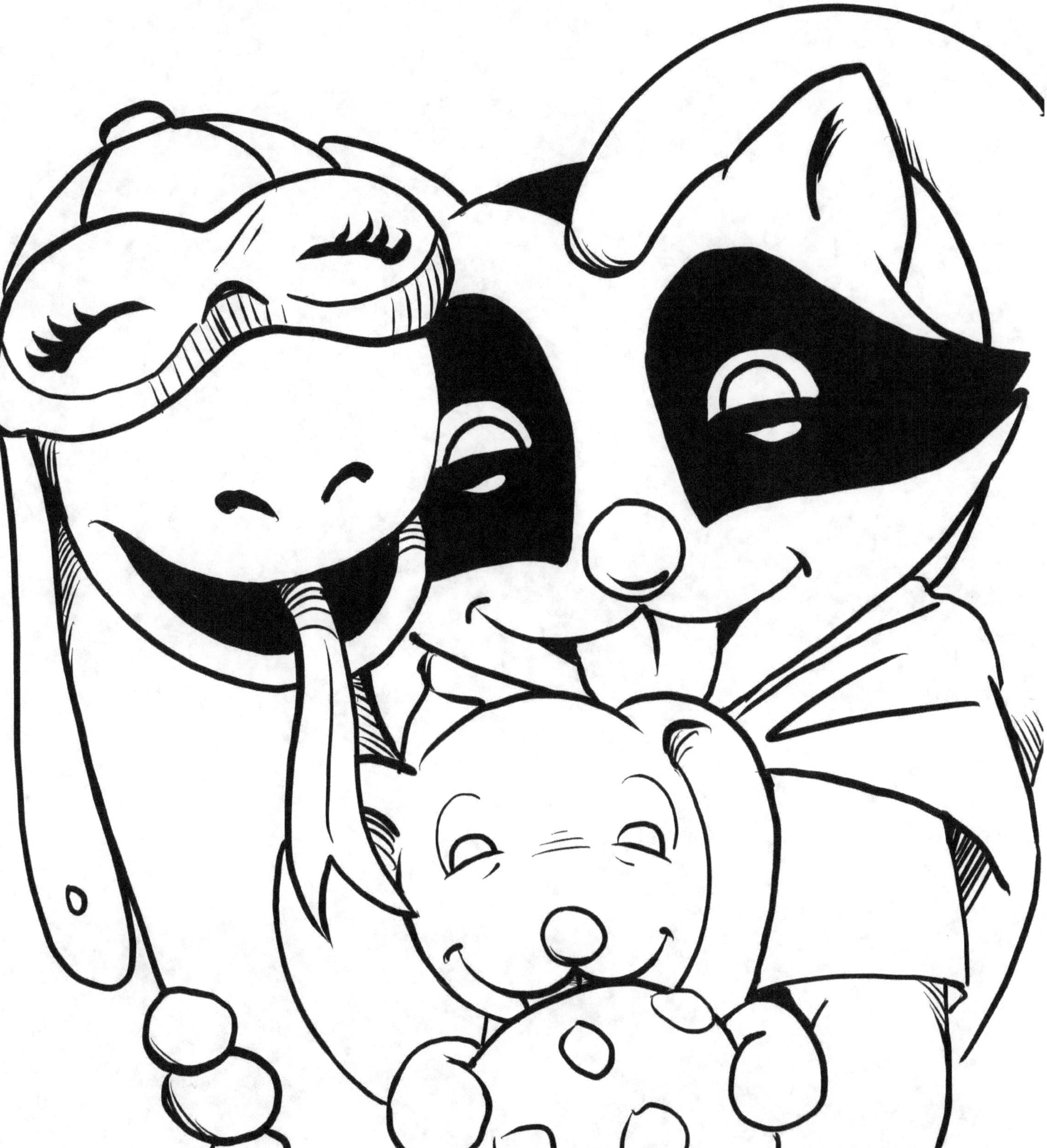

Enjoyed coloring this book?

For more great titles visit:
www.RollingDonutPress.com

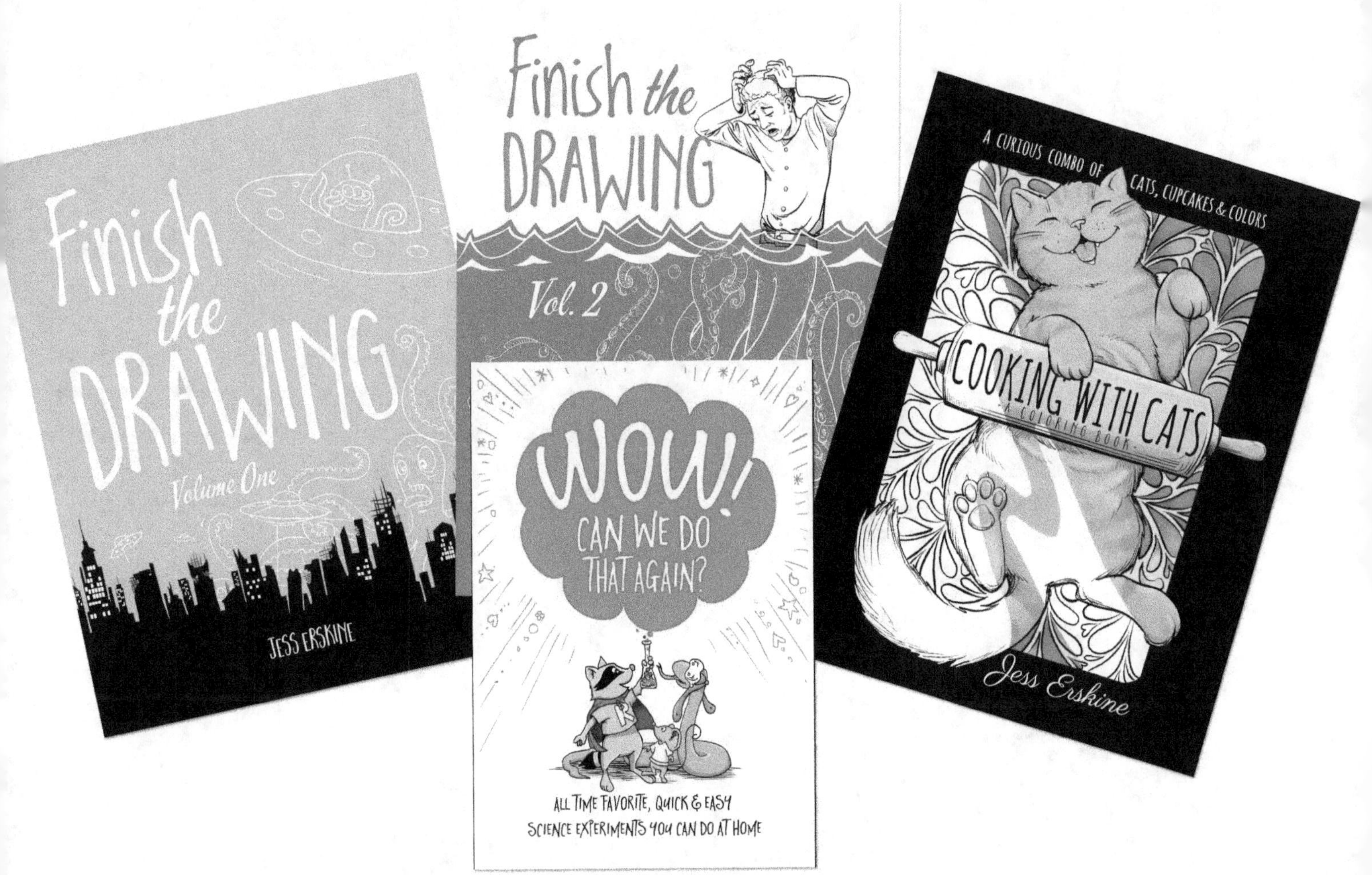

Rolling Donut Press

www.ingramcontent.com/pod-product-compliance
Lightning Source LLC
Chambersburg PA
CBHW081120180526
45170CB00008B/2933